941.44

GLASGOW:
A CITY AT WAR

Brian D. Osborne
and Ronald Armstrong

GLASGOW:
A CITY AT WAR

Birlinn

First published in 2003 by
Birlinn Limited
West Newington House
10 Newington Road
Edinburgh
EH9 1QS

www.birlinn.co.uk

ISBN 1 84158 276 X

British Library Cataloguing-in-Publication Data
A catalogue record for this book is available
from the British Library

Layout and page make up: Mark Blackadder

Printed and bound in Great Britain by the Bath Press, Glasgow

CONTENTS

INTRODUCTION

Glasgow: A City at War in many ways complements our earlier book, *The Clyde at War,* which was published by Birlinn in 2001. As in the earlier volume we have chosen to look at some themes suggested by the subject rather than attempt to provide a comprehensive analysis of every aspect of the topic. Because of the narrowing of our focus in the present book, from the whole Clyde area to the great city that lies at its heart, we have been able to deal in somewhat greater detail with these themes and we hope that even the most knowledgeable lover of Glasgow will find something new and intriguing in both text and pictures.

Each of our thirteen thematic chapters has a block of text and then a selection of what seemed to us the most relevant and interesting photographs that we could find to illustrate the theme. These come from a wide range of sources and each photograph is accompanied by an extended note or explanation.

Glasgow's military tradition, as we hope this book amply demonstrates, is a long and proud one. Her citizens' tradition of opposition to war is also a noteworthy one and we have tried to do justice to this in words and pictures. If, as Georges Clemenceau (amongst others) is supposed to have said, 'war is much too serious a thing to be left to the military', then we have good authority for having devoted considerable space to the impact of war on the non-military population.

In a book devoted to exploring Glasgow's contribution to military matters and the effect of war on the city then it may be interesting to glance briefly at an account of one incident in the city's history when a substantial part of the city's civilian population and the military were engaged in a bitter struggle, a struggle which ended in a tactical withdrawal by the military. The following account of the Shawfield riots of 1725 comes from D. Macleod Malloch's *The Book of Glasgow Anecdote.* (1912).

In 1725 the popular tumult known as the Shawfield Riot took place. In that year the Government imposed a tax on malt; and as home-brewed ale at the time was an indispensable article of common food – the poor man's wine – the tax was highly unpopular. Mr Daniel Campbell of Shawfield was Member of Parliament for the City, and it had become known that he had used his influence in favour of the obnoxious tax. He therefore became an object of popular hatred. When the time came that the impost took effect, there was no small commotion in the town. Crowds of turbulent idlers, chiefly boys and women, collected, who violently hustled the officers charged with carrying out the duty of exacting the tax. Of course the dignity of the law required to be up held, but unfortunately there was no military in the town, and the mob had the best of it. As there was little prospect of a peaceful settlement, two companies of Lord Deloraine's regiment of foot were sent for in hot haste. When the soldiers arrived, Provost Miller ordered the guardhouse to be cleared for their reception; but the doors were locked, and the keys had been carried off, so the soldiers were billeted in the usual way on the householders. Then the Provost and his friends, under the impression that all was over for the time, spent their evening in their tavern or club.

Fourteen years before this time Mr Campbell of Shawfield had built a spacious mansion-house, which, with its great garden, stood upon the site of what is now Glassford Street, then entirely out of the town. As its owner wisely kept out of the way, the mob, having provided themselves with axes, and hammers, proceeded without challenge to demolish the house, the furniture of which they knocked to pieces, with loud shouts of 'Down with Shawfield's house!' 'No malt tax!' Doubtless they would have carried out their threat to pull down the house had not the Provost and Magistrates interfered, and persuaded them to desist. Next day the soldiers obtained possession of the guard-house, which stood on the south-west corner of Candleriggs; but the mob collecting in still greater numbers began to pelt the sentinels with stones. The soldiers were thereupon formed in a hollow square, and were ordered by Captain Bushell, their commander, to fire, which they did, killing two persons. Immediately the rioters broke open the town magazine, took possession of the arms, rang the fire bell, and alarmed the whole town. On the persuasion of the Magistrates, Captain Bushell and his company left the town for Dumbarton Castle; not without a vigorous attack from the enraged citizens. In this riot from first to last nine were killed, and seventeen more or less severely wounded.

ACKNOWLEDGEMENTS

The selection of the most appropriate photographs for a work of this kind was a major task and the picture credits indicate the varied sources we have used and we are grateful to all concerned in obtaining these photographs. We would, however, like to express our thanks, in particular, to a number of people who were exceptionally helpful in our quest for pictures. The excellent images from Yarrows in the 1930s and '40s came at the suggestion of Sir Eric Yarrow and with the considerable help of William Mitchell of BAE Systems, the successors to Yarrows. Two collections at Glasgow Caledonian University – the Kevin Morrison Collection and the William Gallacher Memorial Library – produced a number of fascinating pictures and Kevin Morrison and Audrey Canning, the respective curators, were extremely helpful and interested. Two voluntary bodies, The Rolls Royce Heritage Trust and 602 Squadron Museum, both at Hillington, together ensured that Glasgow's aviation story was well represented. The very rich collection of *The Daily Record* was a major picture source and we are greatly indebted to Catherine Toretti for her interest in the project and her help in accessing these illustrations.

[1]

A PEACEFUL CITY

The Britons of Strathclyde are believed to have commanded a territory that at its peak (around the eighth century) extended from the head of Loch Lomond to Morecambe Bay, and the emerging settlement of Glasgow formed part of their territory. Glasgow's position as one of several fordable points on a shallow river was not of special strategic significance – during the Roman period, for example, it was situated safely within the Antonine Wall. Similarly, Glasgow's Dark-Age settlement had nothing of the importance of Dumbarton (or Alcluith) within the British kingdom. Although a few warrior figures appear in the mythmaking that surrounds Mungo (or Kentigern), Glasgow's subsequent history as told by the chroniclers does not appear to have featured an important military role. Perhaps significantly, the vivid imagery of the city's coat of arms (bell, bird and tree) reflects the founding myth – an unusual one with entirely peaceful symbolism bereft of the usual castles, daggers and other warlike trappings.

Glasgow's rise to prominence within the new Kingdom of Scots was more in an ecclesiastical context – as the seat of a bishop – rather than in a military one, as was the case with the royal burghs of Stirling, Edinburgh or nearby Dumbarton, each with its formidable fortress in a key situation. And as Glasgow entered the medieval period, it remained for the most part on the fringe of stirring national events, well away from the Lothians and the English Plantagenet kings' preferred military route into Scotland. Even so, the great national hero William Wallace probably had some local connections, perhaps with the then Bishop of Glasgow, Robert Wishart. One of the more colourful incidents in William Wallace's campaign of 1297 was his victory in a skirmish with the English or 'Southrons' at the 'Bell o' the Brae' in the upper part of the High Street of Glasgow. The story is told in Blind Harry's narrative poem, *The Wallace*, written in the time of James IV. Blind Harry calls it a skirmish but as the excerpt shows, pretty large numbers of men were involved and the carnage of street-fighting in the narrow High Street can only be imagined. In this passage Harry describes a showdown rather like a scene in a Western film:

Fig. 1

Since classical times at least feats of arms have been celebrated by memorials, often pillars and obelisks, but increasingly in more recent times, sculptured groups of figures. One notable Glasgow example of the latter is the war memorial for the Cameronians, by the Kelvingrove Art Galleries and Museum. The Cameronians (The Scottish Rifles) were closely associated with Glasgow and central Scotland and it was felt appropriate that this striking war memorial commemorating the 7,074 men of the regiment who died in the First World War should be placed in Kelvingrove Park, Glasgow. The bronze group is the work of Philip Lindsay Clark (1889–1977), who himself served as an infantryman in the war and won the DSO. The group shows, in the centre, *(continued overleaf)*

GLASGOW: A CITY AT WAR

Wallace and Boyd up through the plain street go,
The English wondered when they saw no moe.
An ensign was with Beik and Percy there,
Who boldly called, and challenged what they were.
A fierce encounter then, and sharp, between
The Scots and English, as was ever seen,
Quickly ensues, with such a dreadful stint,
Till from their swords the fire flew like flint …

Then Wallace mids that cruel bloody throng,
With his good sword, that heavy was and long.
At the Lord Percy such a stroke he drew,
Till bone and brain in different places flew;
So cruel was the skirmish, and so hot,
The English left seven hundred on the spot.

Tragically for the Scots, Wallace's military career was to come to an end in Glasgow – on 3 August 1305 at Robroyston on the northern outskirts of the modern city. Blind Harry's account of his capture runs:

Robroyston was near the place beside
And but one house where Wallace used to bide …
After midnight in hands they have him tane,
Slumbered on sleep, no man with him but ane.
Keirly they took and led him frae that place.
Did him to death withoutten longer space.

Soon afterwards, as a result of this treachery instigated by 'Fause' Menteith, Wallace was taken on a last fateful journey to trial and execution at Westminster Hall.

While probably the reality was that the city was something of a military and political side-show, there were occasions when Glasgow was at the centre of national events. And even if it was not, historians like the eighteenth-century Glasgow merchant John Gibson contrived to put something of a Glasgow spin onto, for example, events of Scotland's Wars of Independence. Gibson describes the above-mentioned Robert Wishart, Bishop of Glasgow, as a heroic priestly figure very much at the heart of things, a resolute hero standing alongside Robert Bruce in challenging Edward I at the time of the competition for the vacant Scots throne. The speech which Gibson puts into the mouth of the Glasgow bishop seems to anticipate some of the best phrases from the Declaration of Arbroath by about thirty years:

> Scotland from the foundation of the state had been a free and
> independent kingdom, and not subject to any other power
> whatsoever … their ancestors had valiantly defended themselves
> against the Romans, Picts, Britons, Saxons and Danes and all others
> who sought to usurp upon them … all true-hearted Scotsmen will
> stand for the liberty of their country to their deaths; for they esteem
> their liberty to be more precious than their lives, and in that quarrel
> will neither separate nor divide.
>
> Gibson, *History of Glasgow*

Two and a half centuries on, in the later phases of the Reformation in religion, Glasgow was definitely centre-stage in a crucial episode in Scotland's military history. In May 1568, in the final days of the unhappy reign of Mary Queen of Scots, the final and decisive defeat of her forces took place at Langside – on Glasgow's very doorstep. Following her escape from Loch Leven, it was no co-ordinated campaign that brought her and her forces to the south side of the River Clyde at the hilly place now called Mount Florida. Her last throw of the military dice came when her forces reluctantly responded to an attack by Mary's own half-brother, the Regent Moray, from the direction of the city. Even then, Glasgow had not been chosen by the queen's army as a specific strategic target or military objective. Mary herself – and her army with her – was simply intent on moving from the vicinity of one royal castle (Hamilton) to another (Dumbarton). Their line of march brought them to the river, they were taken by surprise, and defeat was overwhelming:

> Here [the queen's forces] were opposed by two battalions of
> spearmen, each presenting a dense rampart; and the struggle was
> fiercely and obstinately contested for upwards of half an hour, those
> of them whose spears were broken drawing their daggers, throwing
> stones, fragments of lances or whatever missile they could lay their
> hands on, in the faces of their enemy. At this crisis some of the rear
> rank of [Moray's] party, whether through cowardice or treachery is
> uncertain, took to flight and would undoubtedly have disordered the
> combatants had not the depth of their array prevented those in front
> from knowing what was occurring in rear. The second division,
> observing the danger, and being themselves disengaged, threw
> forward some entire regiments to the right and reinforced the first
> line. Their adversaries, incapable of withstanding the united attack,

were thrown into irretrievable confusion and universally fled. Urged by hatred and private revenge, the slaughter of the fugitives would have been terrible, had not the Regent sent horsemen in every direction to stop the carnage.

George Buchanan, *History of Scotland*

George Buchanan came from Killearn in Stirlingshire and was tutor to Mary's son, James VI, as well as being a scholar with a European reputation. From his account of the battle we can learn a lot about sixteenth-century warfare, including features such as the 'dense rampart' of spearsmen, which must have resembled the medieval schiltron – so successful when the correct ground had been chosen, as at Bannockburn – so disastrous at Flodden, fifty years before Langside.

During the wars of religion that stained the sixteenth and seventeenth centuries Glasgow again, somehow or other, remained comparatively peaceful. This, even though it was firmly Presbyterian and hostile to the Stewart monarchs' religious policies. The story is often told of how Glasgow's St Mungo's Cathedral escaped the worst excesses of the Reformers, such as those perpetrated in places like St Andrews. In 1579, according to John Gibson again:

Mr Melvil, principal of the college, having for a great while solicited the magistrates to have (the cathedral) pulled down, that at last granted him liberty to do so; but when he, by beat of drum, was assembling the workmen for that purpose, the crafts (who justly looked upon the cathedral as one of the greatest ornaments of their town) ran immediately to arms and informed Mr Melvil that if any person presumed to pull down a single stone of the church, he should, that moment, be buried under it.

So Glasgow's cathedral was able to host the Kirk's General Assembly in November 1638, eight months after the signing of the National Covenant. Almost all present professed various forms of extreme Covenanting zeal and there was open confrontation with Charles I's Commissioner to the Assembly. In a fervid atmosphere the elders and brethren declared the deposition of Charles' bishops and condemned the Prayer Book as 'heathenish, Popish, Jewish and Arminian'. Yet, once more, in the civil wars that followed, Glasgow somehow avoided the kind of slaughter and ruin that was meted out to the hapless citizens of Aberdeen by the Marquis of Montrose's army, or that accompanied the sacking of Dundee by General

Monck. In 1645, during Montrose's *annus mirabilis*, when he came close to Glasgow, on the way to adding Kilsyth to his amazing series of victories, the Glasgow city fathers escaped occupation or a worse fate, at the cost of being requisitioned for a number of bonnets and shoes.

In June 1679, during the reign of Charles II, the Tolbooth of Glasgow was fortified by troops of John Graham of Claverhouse, known to his followers as 'Bonnie Dundee' and to his opponents, including many townsfolk of Glasgow, as 'Bluidy Clavers'. Claverhouse had taken up his position at the Market Cross and had thrown up barricades across the High Street, the Gallowgate and the Saltmarket. The opposing Covenanting force – fresh from a victory at Drumclog – was put to flight by his dragoons. Later in the same month, the Battle of Bothwell Brig took place within half a day's march of the city. Many sympathisers went out from Glasgow to fight on the Covenanting side, and many failed to return. The Covenanting army, large in numbers, though fatally divided in policy, aims and leadership, mustered at Bothwell Bridge near Hamilton and confronted a government force under the Duke of Monmouth. The latter won an easy victory with around 600 Covenanting casualties and 1,200 prisoners taken.

The Jacobites found little favour from the city of Glasgow. No support was forthcoming in the '15 Rebellion and in the '45 Charles Edward Stewart took the city without opposition in December 1745, having entered the city on Christmas Day by way of the Back Cow Loan (now Ingram Street). What sort of reception could the Highland Host expect? Or more importantly – what fate would be meted out to Glaswegians?

> The city of Glasgow, upon which Charles was now in full march, had much greater reason than Dumfries, or even Lesmahagow, to expect severe treatment from the insurgents; while its wealth gave additional cause for alarm, without in the least degree supplying better means of defence. This city, newly sprung into importance, had never required nor received the means of defence, but was now lying, with its widespread modern streets and well-stored warehouses, fully exposed to the licence of the invaders. It had distinguished itself, ever since the expulsion of the House of Stuart, by its attachment to the new [Hanoverian] government; and since the Highlanders entered England, had with gratuitous loyalty, raised a regiment of 1200 men, to aid in suppressing the insurrection.
>
> *History of the Rebellion of 1745–6*

As this passage suggests, it might have been expected that the Highland army would pillage or otherwise do great harm to the city, but this simply did not happen – even though the majority of the citizens were convinced Whigs. Cameron of Lochiel it was, or so the story goes, who saved the city from destruction:

> … a resolution had been taken by the rebels to plunder and burn the city of Glasgow, and had not [Lochiel] threatened to withdraw his clan [Clan Cameron] if this resolution should be put in practice, it is probable that Glasgow would have been destroyed.
>
> Gibson, *History of Glasgow*

What the Young Pretender did was: stay for eight days, create a flurry among the younger element of young ladies – something more than a flurry in the case of one Clementina Walkinshaw – and, rather as Montrose had done exactly 100 years before, confront the city magistrates with a demand for the complete refitting of his army. The requisition explicitly demanded 12,000 shirts, 6,000 cloth coats, 6,000 pairs of stockings, and 6,000 pairs of shoes. Following that, the prince sought to put fresh heart into the whole campaign by reviewing his troops at Flesher's Haugh near the Glasgow Green.

> We marched out, with drums beating, colours flying, bagpipes playing, and all the marks of a triumphant army to the appointed ground, attended by multitudes of people, who had come from all parts to see us, and especially the ladies, who, though formerly much against us, were now charmed by the sight of the Prince into the most enthusiastic loyalty.
>
> Captain Daniel's Memoir

In fact only sixty citizens followed the Jacobite cause, donned the white cockade and marched out to face defeat at Culloden Moor, less than four months later.

Culloden, the last battle fought on British soil, was first celebrated as a victory and then quickly forgotten by Hanoverian Glasgow, many miles to the south. Very swiftly too the pursuit of trade and commerce was resumed by its citizens. Glasgow's location in the west of the country, with good and improving access to the Clyde estuary, and in time the Atlantic, made it ripe for trading success, soon to be followed by industrial success. Political union with England meant that any wars were likely to be far-off wars of empire, although the city's swelling population and fluctuating employment were fresh reasons for the Scottish (or Glasgow) soldier to rally to the colours.

General Wolfe of Quebec may not have been specifically referring to the Glasgow regiments when he commented 'it was no great mischief if they fall', but there were others who held a similar view of the Glasgow soldiery. The Glasgow regiments became not so much soldiers of fortune, as the willing servants of the British armed forces' imperial role. With the growing incorporation of Glasgow and Scotland into a United Kingdom, with the blurring of the age-old line of demarcation, with the emergence of a world-wide British empire (and Glasgow as its 'Second City'), the distinctiveness of the Scottish soldier – the tartan, the trews and the pipes – provided a valuable and convenient emblem of individuality and identity.

The rise of trade and industry made Glasgow well fitted to establish links with America, through tobacco and then cotton. Even though Glasgow regiments were prominent in the failed struggle to keep the Americans within the imperial ambit, and the Royal Scots Fusiliers burned the White House in 1812 (and consumed a meal set out for the Congressmen), there were strong links between elements of opinion within the city and the USA. Several blockade-runners in the American Civil War were in fact Clyde-built steamers. The shipbuilders of Glasgow and the Clyde, from the time of Robert Napier's Govan shipyard and the *Black Prince* – the first warship built on the Clyde for the Admiralty – provided a growing number of vessels for the Royal Navy, and indeed other navies around the world. Glasgow, as one of the workshops of the new industrial age, became increasingly dependent on the armaments industry. As the city moved into the twentieth century, the locomotive builders in the city's north side, for example, diversified to produce vast quantities of shells and artillery. Such diversification was in part an attempt to stave off the lurking economic depression that was never far away – the collapse of the City of Glasgow Bank in 1879 being just one indicator of this.

The Boer War was the last and perhaps the quintessential imperialist war, but there were times when sabre-rattling began to pall and at such times the Glasgow public could exhibit a measure of support for the underdog. Neil Munro's Erchie MacPherson alludes to this unexpected sympathy for the enemy in a *Glasgow Evening News* story of 23 June:

> Oh aye, it's a grand thing peace, as ony married man'll tell ye. Twa years ago, the chaps that sends the things to the newspapers couldna find words bad enough to describe the treachery and bloodthirstiness and cowardice of the Boers. The mair he bate us, the mair o' a blackguard he wiz; but noo that we hiv bate him, he hiz become the boldest, bravest, maist honourable foeman ever cocked a gun. Maybe

Fig. 2

William Wallace, who won an important battle against English forces at the Bell o' the Brae in 1297. This was probably an early example of street fighting. The portrait is described as being 'from an ancient painting in the possession of Sir John Maxwell of Pollok'.

Fig. 3

Mary, Queen of Scots lost the Battle of Langside in 1568 on the outskirts of Glasgow.

he picked up a' thae virtues between the times he wiz jinkin' us roond the barbed wire fences. Onywye, the Boer and Tommy is noo swappin' socks on the veldt like brithers born, and trying to dae each other in the bargain; and the war correspondents is cablin' hame poems describin' the love which thae twa hae for ane anither noo, and the only folk that's vext the row's a' by is the Irish.

The Treaty of Vereeniging, which ended the war was, largely due to Lord Kitchener, unexpectedly moderate in some of its terms. And, some years later, on September 2 1914, Glasgow was able to look back on a whole decade of peace. In the First World War however, the early burst of patriotic enthusiasm that sent young Glaswegians flocking to the recruiting offices was proportionately greater than in other parts of the UK – 30,000 in the first ten weeks of hostilities, or the equivalent of every able-bodied male from nineteen to twenty-four years of age. In the years that followed their enthusiasm would be put to the severest of tests.

As a postscript to this introductory chapter which has looked at Glasgow's military involvement through history up to the eve of The First World War, here is part of a poem written by Katherine Mann, which draws a picture of the most celebrated Glasgow battle, Langside – the defeat in 1568 of Mary Queen of Scots. The poem was written in 1918 to mark the 350 anniversary, and skilfully merges aspects of the battle with the much greater twentieth-century conflict ('Once more to arms'):

The Queen of Scots at Langside

Three hundred years and fifty gone!
Yet closer to you now than then,
O Mary, by war's sorrows drawn,
Since you rode through by Rutherglen.

And as you scanned the battle slopes
In that dire hour predestinate,
We feel again your beating hopes,
Again we watch the scales of fate.

Once more to arms – but ruthless fray!
Through ours we see your vanguard sweep,
And as you prayed we also pray,
And for our sons like vigil keep.

We too with destiny contend,
O fairest and ill-fortuned Queen,
With full hearts now to comprehend
The pang, the anguish yours had been.

More deep, more deep your griefs to sear –
Since on yon hill your banner fell –
Than ours whose hosts to victory veer,
Whose drums roll out the despot's knell.

Fig. 4

Langside, Glasgow, where
in May 1568 the army of
Mary, Queen of Scots was
finally defeated by the
forces of Regent Moray,
the queen's own half-
brother. The present day
memorial to the battle of
Langside stands among the
douce surroundings of the
Victorian suburb of the
same name.

GLASGOW: A CITY AT WAR

Fig. 5

The High Street of Glasgow as it may have looked during the Covenanting Wars, when 'Bluidy Clavers' dragoons fought a skirmish there in June 1679. The royalist troops of John Graham of Claverhouse, known to his supporters as 'Bonnie Dundee', defeated a force of Covenanters and drove them out of the city. Despite this, most of Glasgow was very much on the side of the defeated force.

Fig. 6

Prince Charles Edward Stewart came to Glasgow in December 1745, after his retreat from Derby. He reviewed his troops on the green.

Fig. 7

HMS *Black Prince*, built by Napier. *Black Prince* was launched from Robert Napier's Govan shipyard on 27 February 1861. She was a 9,000-ton iron steam frigate, built for the Royal Navy as part of the response to the challenge posed by the French ironclad *La Gloire*, launched in 1859. *Black Prince* was armed with 34 muzzle-loading cannon firing 68-lb balls arranged on one gun-deck – hence her rather strange designation as a frigate, despite her being much heavier than any of the three-decked line of battle ships which still made up the main strength of the British fleet. Although her engines produced 1,250 horsepower, the conservatism of her designers and Admiralty policy dictated that she should still be rigged in the same way as the old battle ships. Not until full rigging could be eliminated would it become practical to design ships with central, turret-mounted guns. Earlier ironclad ships – including vessels such as the monitor *Erebus* built by Napier during the Crimean War – had been little more than floating batteries designed to reduce Russian fortifications. As far back as 1843, just after Robert Napier had acquired an iron-shipbuilding facility with his new yard at Govan, the firm had won a Royal Navy contract for three iron gunboats – *Jackal, Lizard* and *Bloodhound* – which were to be the Navy's first iron-built ships. The significance of the *Black Prince* contract lay in the recognition of the Clyde and Napier as major Admiralty contractors and the development of the principle of using commercial yards as the main suppliers of naval ships. *Black Prince*, which was renamed *Emerald* in 1903 and *Impregnable III* in 1910, survived until 1923 – the latter part of her life being spent in various training roles. *(US Naval Historical Center)*

GLASGOW: A CITY AT WAR

Fig. 8
Soldiers of the Springburn Artillery relax in an off-duty moment with a barrel of ale. They have probably been playing football.
(The Mitchell Library, Glasgow)

Fig. 9
A view of the Gordon Highlanders being presented with new colours at Glasgow's Maryhill Barracks before relations and friends in the years before the First World War. Maryhill Barracks was completed in 1872 to replace the old infantry barracks (built in 1795) in the Gallowgate.
(The Mitchell Library, Glasgow)

Fig. 10
A group photograph of blacksmiths, farriers and cavalry soldiers belonging to the Royal Scots Greys at Maryhill Barracks. Cavalry regiments needed a small army of back-up personnel to look after the horses. Note the small child, who probably lived in married quarters. *(The Mitchell Library, Glasgow)*

[2]
THE PEOPLE IN ARMS

There has been a long tradition of voluntary response to problems of national defence and the Local Defence Volunteers and Home Guards of the Second World War represent only one example of this response – albeit a very large-scale one in terms of numbers engaged and a very significant one in terms of the contribution to national solidarity and social cohesion. The concept of 'The People's War' is certainly one with much relevance to the war of 1939 to 1945: the mass involvement of the civilian population in civil and military defence measures is one distinguishing feature of this war, even when compared to the war of 1914 to 1918.

It is a remarkable fact that the Home Guard in June 1941 commanded the services of almost 20 per cent of the adult male civilian population who were not otherwise engaged in police or civil defence duties. None of the earlier volunteer movements had ever attracted support on this level. The Home Guard peaked at a total of 1.8 million volunteers in March 1943 and remained at a strength of over a million until it was disbanded. Though certainly the largest and the most popular of all the volunteer movements, it was by no means the first.

In the days of the war with Revolutionary France, Glasgow responded to the external threat and perceived internal threats with enthusiasm. James Cleland in his *Annals of Glasgow* wrote:

> The revolutionary principles of France had made such rapid progress in this country, that an Act of Parliament was passed, authorising his Majesty to accept the military services of such of his loyal subjects as chose to enrol themselves as Volunteers, for the defence of our inestimable constitution. The necessary arrangements had no sooner been made, than a number of citizens of Glasgow offered their services to Government, which was immediately accepted, under the denomination of the Royal Glasgow Volunteers.

The 300 rank-and-file Royal Glasgow Volunteers, raised in 1794, served

Fig. 11
The enthusiasm with which the Home Guard tackled their role can be seen in this photograph from the Glasgow training centre. Note that two of the men are armed with the Sten gun, which was issued in very large numbers to the Home Guard.
(Imperial War Museum)

without pay, provided their own uniforms and elected their officers by ballot. A second Regiment of Loyal Glasgow Volunteers – 800 strong – followed in 1797, but they, presumably being drawn from a less affluent part of the population, received pay and clothing and their officers were appointed by public bodies. In the same year the Royal Glasgow Volunteer Light Horse was raised, sixty men who found their own mounts, uniforms and equipment and elected their officers.

These volunteers and the Armed Association served until the Peace of Amiens of April 1802 brought a pause in the war. When war resumed in May 1803 a new wave of volunteer regiments was raised.

1803 Volunteer Units

REGIMENT	STATUS	STRENGTH	NOTES
1st Regiment of Glasgow Volunteers	Paid	800	
2nd Regiment, or Trades' House Volunteer Infantry	Unpaid	600	All master tradesmen
3rd Regiment, or Highland Volunteers	Paid	600	Two companies of Sharp-shooters served without pay
4th Regiment, or Sharp-shooters	Unpaid	500	
5th Regiment, or Grocers' Corps	Unpaid	300	
Anderston Volunteer Corps	Paid	500	
Armed Association	Unpaid	240	
Canal Volunteer Corps	Paid	240	
Royal Glasgow Volunteer Light Horse	Unpaid	70	

These units, apart from regular drills and training, were embodied for a one-month period of permanent duty each year.

In 1808 a Local Militia Act was passed and Glasgow's colourful variety of Volunteer Regiments were subsumed into four battalions of the Lanarkshire Local Militia, each of ten companies and 700 rank and file.

All these units were intended for home defence, for the control of civil disturbance and enabled the release of regular, and second line, Fencible, units for active service. With the coming of peace in 1815 the Local Militia was stood down, the men discharged and their arms returned to Government depots.

In the mid-nineteenth century fears of a French invasion awoke concerns about many aspects of national defence (one manifestation being the construction of the iron-clad *Black Prince* – see Chapter 1) including the re-awakening of interest in a volunteer movement to supplement and reinforce the regular army.

The famous review of the Scottish Volunteers by Queen Victoria in Holyrood Park, Edinburgh on 25 August 1881 has, by reason of the remarkably inclement weather, gone down in history as the 'Wet Review'. Sixty years later obituaries in local newspapers across Scotland could still be found reporting that the late Mr X was 'a veteran of the 'Wet Review'.

The Volunteer Movement tended often to be fairly bourgeois in character (certainly in its officer corps) and many of the volunteers enjoyed the social aspects of the movement. The Springburn Artillerymen whose photograph appears in Chapter 1 were clearly enjoying the comradeship of the service. Scottish volunteers regularly featured in the Queen's Prize rifle shooting competition at Bisley.

The Volunteers were absorbed into the Territorial Army – or, as it was initially known, the Territorial Force – in the reforms introduced in the 1907 Territorial and Reserve Forces Act by the Liberal Secretary of State for War Richard Haldane (1856–1928). The Territorial Force was intended for home defence purposes but, as was mentioned in Chapter 1, Territorial Force battalions were swiftly called upon for foreign service on the outbreak of war in 1914.

The outbreak of war in August 1914 saw a great wave of patriotic emotion overtake the city and an outlet for this was sought by many who were, for various reasons, unable to enlist in the Regular Army or the Territorials. A military training association – the Citizen Training Force – was established. Twelve companies were to be established in various locations across Glasgow – and another company arranged to drill in the city centre at 5.30 p.m. The Citizen Training Force volunteers were committed to two drills per week and on alternate weeks would take part in battalion drill, a march out or a field exercise. By November the Glasgow Citizen Training Force had 4,000 members and Colonel John Shaughnessy, lately commanding officer of the 7th Scottish Rifles (the former 3rd Lanark Rifle Volunteers), had been appointed to command the new formation.

The War Office did not encourage the formation of the CTF although they were allowed to use Territorial Force drill halls. The CTF initially recruited those whose business or family commitments prevented their enlistment for full-time service but it also saw its role as encouraging recruitment into the Imperial Forces.

Neil Munro reveals something of the character of the CTF in his newspaper column recounting the adventures of a Glasgow commercial traveller, Jimmy Swan. Jimmy describes the personnel of the Force and the demands that their instructor, Sergeant Watson, made on the volunteers:

> … I wish he would mind at times our corps' no' made up o' gladiators or Græco-Roman wrestlers, that we're just plain business men, off and on about five-and-forty in the shade, wi' twenty years o' tramway travellin' and elevator lifts, and easy-chairs, bad air and beer in our constitution. It's no to be expected we can pelt up braes on the Fenwick Road like a lot o' laddies.

> … Sergeant Watson's system's gey sore on the muscles for a week or two, but it's most morally elevatin'. Four weeks ago if I had attempted to lean on mysel' wi' any weight I would have crumpled up like a taper; I'm sore all over just at present, but I feel that I could take a cow by the tail and swing it round my head …

The Force continued through 1915, becoming known as the Glasgow Volunteer Force in September that year. In March 1915 Colonel Shaugnnessy got command of a Territorial battalion and was replaced as CO by Lt-Col. John Dodds, late the 5th Battalion Highland Light Infantry (Territorial Force). In April 1915 2,000 men of the Force paraded in Victoria Park. Colonel Dodds noted that 'the men were steady on parade, performed the movements correctly, and with intelligence and discrimination'. A larger turnout at this parade had been expected but, due to a Regular Army route march, the city's tramcar service had been interrupted.

The position of the Force was regularised in February 1916 by the Government's extension of the provisions of the Volunteers Act of 1863 to it. Two battalions of what was to be known as the City of Glasgow Volunteer Regiment were authorised under Colonel Sir Archibald McInnes Shaw as County Commandant. A third battalion was authorised in October 1916, all three battalions being formed from the personnel of the Glasgow Volunteer Force.

The duties of the Volunteers were defined in a War Office statement. They would only be called out for actual military service if and when it became necessary to repel the enemy in the event of an invasion being imminent. However they could be given the responsibility for guarding vulnerable points and lines of communication, thus releasing Regular and Territorial Force units for active service.

In the years before the outbreak of the Second World War steps were taken to create a civilian defence network of air-raid wardens, volunteer fire-fighters, ambulance drivers, etc. – a story told in Chapters 3 and 4. No steps were taken to create any part-time military training force – although the strength of the Territorial Army was doubled in Spring 1939 and conscription was introduced.

When Neville Chamberlain resigned as Prime Minister in May 1940 one of the first steps taken by the new government was to seek to raise a volunteer force to help defend Britain from the threat of invasion. The 'phoney war' in France had gone critical with the German blitzkrieg rolling through Holland, Belgium and France.

The new Secretary of State for War, Anthony Eden, broadcast to the nation on 14 May 1940 and asked for volunteers:

> We want large numbers of such men in Great Britain who are British subjects, between the ages of seventeen and sixty-five, to come forward now and offer their services in order to make assurance [of successfully repelling an invasion] doubly sure. The name of the new force which is now to be raised will be the Local Defence Volunteers. This name describes its duties in three words. You will not be paid, but you will receive uniforms and will be armed. In order to volunteer, what you have to do is give your name at your local police station, and then, when we want you, we will let you know …

The Government's expectation was that perhaps 150,000 might come forward as a first response to Eden's broadcast – however 250,000 men had put their names down for the Local Defence Volunteers within 24 hours. By the end of the month over 300,000 volunteers were enrolled and by the end of June there were 1,456,000 registered volunteers. In July 1940 the LDV was renamed the Home Guard on the instructions of Prime Minister Winston Churchill, who felt that the original name was less than inspiring.

Glasgow shared in the national enthusiasm with six sub-groups established by May in the Central, Marine, Southern, Northern, Maryhill and Govan police divisions. The LDV (and later the Home Guard) were of course all-male organisations – a matter which caused disappointment in some female circles. Venetia Foster went so far as to set up an Amazon Defence Corps, based in London, with the aim of training women in the use of rifles – Mrs Foster, the wife of a naval officer, said, 'we hope in time to persuade the Government to let us serve with the LDV'. No parallel movement was reported from Glasgow.

The new movement caused some unhappiness with existing organisations

GLASGOW: A CITY AT WAR

– in Glasgow there was a degree of tension between the LDV commander and the Chief Constable, Sir Percy Sillitoe. There had been cases of LDV men holding up police and ARP wardens and asking for identity papers and the LDV commander claimed that he had ultimate responsibility for Glasgow's safety. Sillitoe wrote in his memoirs:

> ... as long as Civil Law continued to function within the city of Glasgow I would not accept 'instructions' regarding my police duties and responsibilities from any military authority.

The LDV and the Home Guard were initially burdened with a structure of oddly-named ranks and insignia – 'battalion commander' instead of lieutenant colonel and stripes of blue braid to indicate officer ranks rather than the army's usual pips and crowns – but in February 1941 Home Guard ranks were aligned with army ranks and shoulder flashes replaced arm bands – the early denim overalls were already being replaced with army battledress.

Many of the LDVs or Home Guards were veterans of the 1914–18 war and the higher levels of command were generally occupied by senior ex-officers. Indeed the hardly-radical *Glasgow Herald* noted in April 1941 that when the War Office released the names of 319 senior commanders in the Home Guard who were to receive commissions under the new arrangements there were 'only 19 plain Misters'. The rest were made up of generals, colonels, peers, knights, etc. The British class system would survive even the shock of war.

One of the problems facing the new force was the great shortage of arms and equipment. When the British Expeditionary Force was evacuated from Dunkirk in May 1940 it left behind much of its equipment, vehicles, stores and ammunition. The re-equipment of the regular forces was the first call on the armaments industry and initially the Local Defence Volunteers were armed with a heterogeneous collection of sporting rifles, shotguns, pikes, and home-made incendiary bombs – the famous Molotov cocktail. Several hundred thousand obsolete American and Canadian rifles – in what was for the British Army a non-standard 0.300 calibre – were imported for the LDV and recruitment had to be restricted to match the availability of supplies. As late as May 1941 not all Home Guardsmen had received a steel helmet.

New weapons, some of slightly dubious utility, which could be cheaply produced without diverting traditional arms manufacturing from the re-supply of front-line troops, or which could be imported from the United States, were made available to the Home Guard. Thus the Spigot Mortar and the Northover Projector were produced to give Home Guard units some support capacity and the Thompson sub-machine gun, beloved of Chicago gangsters, increased the firepower of infantry units. The basic, cheap, but highly effective Sten gun was introduced into Home Guard service and by 1943 almost a quarter of a million examples of this economical weapon, which was said to cost only 35s. (£1.75) to manufacture, were in Home Guard hands.

The Home Guard units in Glasgow worked hard and took part in many exercises to test their capabilities and train them in the realities of modern war. In October 1941 thousands of Home Guards defended the city against regular troops. The Chief Umpire for the exercise was reported by the *Glasgow Herald* to say:

> The advancing columns were held up very satisfactorily by the Home Guard. I am satisfied that forces such as were represented in the exercise would, provided the Home Guard held their dispositions properly, be very seriously delayed, and that the casualties inflicted would be so considerable that an enemy would be very lucky to reach important parts of the city.

Of course not every exercise went entirely smoothly. In November of the same year regular army Special Services troops – as the new Commando units were then known – were set to attack a Govan factory defended by D Co., 5th Battalion, Glasgow Home Guard. Unfortunately the defenders were not at full strength as many of them had been unable to reach the factory due to a bus strike.

One difficulty faced by the Home Guard nationwide, and particularly acutely in Glasgow, was the growing feeling that a German invasion was not actually very likely. In the weeks and months after Dunkirk – during the Battle of Britain period – there was a perception that if control of the skies were lost an invasion was possible; and as we now know the Germans had indeed planned 'Operation Sealion' – the invasion of England – but postponed it indefinitely in mid-September 1940. With the invasion of the Soviet Union in June 1941 it became less and less likely that a cross-Channel adventure would be attempted, and the prospects of the Wehrmacht marching up the Gallowgate became less and less credible. Victory was certainly not in sight at the end of 1941, but the chances of invasion, or final defeat, were certainly receding and with the entry of the United States into the war a growing confidence in victory was evident.

This had its impact on Home Guard morale – but still large numbers of men turned out for regular drills and periodic large-scale exercises. As time went on and the invasion threat receded, issues arose which would have not perhaps been aired during the nervous days of 1940. In May 1942 the Convener of the Church of Scotland's Church and Nation Committee, the Rev. Matthew Stewart of Hamilton, raised concerns about the frequency of Home Guard training exercises and noted that in some areas it was found possible to arrange these for Sunday afternoons or one Sunday morning in two – but in other areas every Sunday morning was devoted to military exercises, thus depriving the Guardsmen the opportunity to attend church.

In 1943 it was agreed that Home Guards working long hours at civilian occupations could ease off routine drills when adequately trained. In April 1943 the *Glasgow Herald* ran a story entitled 'Home Guard's Role When Allies Invade', which explored the changing role of the Home Guard, formed originally to counter an invasion threat but increasingly seen as a force which could take on security tasks in order to free regular units to form part of the army which would eventually land in Europe, liberate the occupied countries and take the war to Hitler's homeland.

One area where the Home Guard soon found a new role was in manning anti-aircraft batteries. Large numbers of regular troops were used in Anti-Aircraft Command and being able to comb some of them out for re-deployment to other combat duties was an obviously attractive prospect for a manpower-hungry military machine. A particularly heavy utilisation of Home Guards in Glasgow was in their role in the surprisingly little known 'Z' Rocket Batteries.

The Home Guard Anti-Aircraft batteries were formed in Spring 1942 and 101 Glasgow Home Guard 'Z' Battery was created and linked to the regular 107 'Z' Battery Royal Artillery, which was located at Prospecthill Road near Mount Florida.

The 'Z' rocket (sometimes known by its codename of UP – unrotated projectile) was a 3-inch solid fuel rocket with a 4.25 lb high explosive warhead. They were variously fitted in single, twin or nine-barrelled mountings. The 'Z' rockets were normally fired under radar direction. They were not highly accurate but fired in salvoes made an undoubtedly impressive and probably effective means of discouraging enemy aircraft.

Major J.B. Murray commanded 101 Battery, which had been formed at a football match at the nearby Hampden Park – where a parade was held and conditions of service broadcast. The establishment of the battery might at first seem astonishingly large – 49 officers and 1,395 other ranks – but of course the Home Guards had full-time jobs and could only reasonably be expected to man their rocket projectors on a rota basis. Some 900 volunteers had come forward by August 1941 but this was inadequate and the Labour

Exchanges had to direct men into the unit. This mixing of volunteers and 'pressed men' had implications for morale and led to attendance problems; the Battery's absenteeism rate at times reached 20 per cent. A better arrangement was reached in 1943 when 101 Battery was linked to 3rd Glasgow Battalion of the Home Guard – the infantry unit was used to feed men into the Anti-Aircraft unit as the invasion threat receded.

The 101 Battery was the first Home Guard unit in Scotland to man rocket projectors and by August 1943 90 per cent of the rocket projectors on the Prospecthill Road site were Home Guard manned. The Battery only saw action on one occasion – on 25 March 1943 German aircraft were engaged at 00.43 a.m. and sixty rounds fired. One enemy aircraft was destroyed but, as other 'Z' batteries and heavy anti-aircraft guns were engaged, the credit for the 'kill' was shared by the area rather than the unit. The duty officer who commanded the battery on this occasion was Captain I.H.C. Williams o.c. 4 Sub Battery (Thursday).

A second 'Z' battery was created in October 1942 and sited at Balornock in the north of the city – the battery later moved to Blackhill and was operational by spring 1943. This unit – 102 Battery – was linked to the 2nd Glasgow Home Guard Battalion and was commanded by Major G. Booth. In July 1943 it retrained and re-equipped with nine-barrelled projectors – four such projectors were manned in July – a number that rose to an average of ten projectors in April/May 1944. The 102 Battery was never called upon to go into action.

The modest operational activity of these two units was of course due to the very limited extent of German air attacks on the Glasgow area after the March – May 1941 series of raids – such as the Clydebank blitz of 13/14 March and the Greenock blitz of 5/6 May.

Although most of the Home Guard effort in anti-aircraft defence went into the 'Z' batteries (which were re-named 'rocket batteries' in May 1944) some Home Guard units manned more conventional anti-aircraft guns. In the Glasgow area a section of two 3.7-inch heavy anti-aircraft guns was manned by A Troop of 71st Clyde Heavy Anti-Aircraft Battery. The officers and men forming A Troop were transferred from 5th Glasgow Home Guard Battalion and most of them had been in the Home Guard Company formed from the workers of G. & J. Weir's engineering works in Cathcart.

The two Glasgow rocket batteries, two rocket batteries in Renfrewshire, one in Dumbartonshire and two Home Guard heavy anti-aircraft batteries were all controlled by 21st Home Guard Anti-Aircraft Regiment. This regiment had an authorised strength of 396 officers and 9,998 men and its actual strength at stand-down was 308 officers and 8,179 men. The number

GLASGOW: A CITY AT WAR

of men involved in Home Guard anti-aircraft duties in the Glasgow area was thus very large and, although the circumstances of the war meant that few saw much action, their work was nonetheless highly significant. It is perhaps surprising that so little of it has remained in the public memory – the 'Dad's Army' image of amateur infantrymen being unfairly dominant.

After the Normandy landings of June 1944 took the war to the continent of Europe, the role of the Home Guard became more and more problematical and compulsory drills and duties were ended in September. It was finally decided to stand-down the Home Guard in December and parades took place on 3 December throughout the country. King George VI, who had become Colonel-in-Chief of the Home Guard, took the salute at Hyde Park, London, where he said in an address to the Home Guard:

> You have discovered in yourselves new capabilities. You have found how men from all types of homes and many different occupations can work together in a great cause and how happy they can be with each other.
>
> That is a memory and a knowledge which may help us all in the many peace-time problems we shall have to tackle before long.
>
> I am very proud of what the Home Guard has done and I give my heartfelt thanks to you all.

Fig. 13

A Glasgow Area Town Fighting School was established to train the Home Guard in the art of house-to-house fighting. This photograph, from 1942, shows local Guardsmen being put through their paces at the training centre.
(*Imperial War Museum*)

Fig. 14

A hero of the 1914–18 War – Major General Dudley Graham Johnson, VC, inspects Glasgow Home Guardsmen at the Dixon's Blazes training centre. Major General Johnson had won his VC while commanding the 2nd Battalion The Royal Sussex Regiment at the crossing of the Sambre Canal in November 1918. After a distinguished career he became Inspector of Infantry from 1941 to 1944.
(*Imperial War Museum*)

Fig. 15

Although most Home Guard units were raised on a geographical basis many large industrial concerns sustained their own Home Guard company or platoon. This photograph shows the platoon formed from the workers at the Yarrow's shipyard, on parade at the company's recreation grounds. The variety of equipment used by the Home Guard is well illustrated in this photograph. On the left, lying prone, is a two-man Bren-gun team – their Bren-gun is fitted with a 100-round circular box magazine. On the right is a Vickers machine gun team – the box on the ground contains water for the cooling mechanism. Behind the machine gunners can be seen a number of Guardsmen carrying Sten sub-machine-guns and in the middle a private armed with an EY rifle grenade launcher, which fired a Type 36 hand grenade.
(BAE Systems)

Fig. 16

A demonstration of the 'Z' rocket projector for Scottish newspaper editors at a site 'somewhere in Scotland' in September 1943. There were two 'Z' batteries manned by the Home Guard in the north and south of Glasgow. The 'Z' rocket was 6 ft 4 in. long, weighed 54 lb and had a 4.25 lb high explosive warhead. It reached a speed of 1,500 feet per second and had an operational ceiling of 20,000 feet. *(Imperial War Museum)*

Fig. 17

A mass barrage of Z rockets being fired for the press demonstration in September 1943. An impressive sight and one that would have surely deterred any German pilot from pressing home his attack.
(Imperial War Museum)

Fig. 18

The Home Guard was 'stood-down' in November 1944. Parades were held throughout the country to mark the end of service of this remarkable volunteer force. Our photograph shows some of the 10,000 men of the Glasgow battalions of the Home Guard marching past a saluting stand in George Square on Sunday 3 December – Lord Provost James Welsh is taking the salute along with Brigadier J.W.L.S. Hobart, Commander of the Glasgow Sub-District of the Home Guard. *(The Daily Record)*

[3]
THE FIRST WORLD WAR

Trouble in far corners of Europe in the summer of 1914 seemed unlikely to have much impact on the bustling life of Glasgow and few people setting off on their Fair Holidays or the city's Territorials going off to their annual camp at Gailes or Troon (see Chapter 9) suspected that their secure and seemingly stable world was about to be turned upside down in a few weeks.

When war was declared on 4 August 1914 there was an immediate patriotic rush to enlist in the Armed Forces or to find other means of service. While Britain was not in fact unprepared for war, the Navy's capital ships especially having been built up over the past few years, she had a relatively small professional army, and that army was scattered, keeping watch over a vast world-wide empire. The need to enlarge the army and to equip and arm these new recruits for a European war was a huge undertaking, with significant local impact. Some idea of the scale of change is given by the size of the British Expeditionary Force on the Western Front. This rose from 120,000 men in 1914 to 2,500,000 in 1918 – around a 21-fold increase. There was a commensurate increase in the number of artillery pieces and a vastly greater increase in mechanised transport. Although a battleship-building programme had been underway since the launch of HMS *Dreadnought* in 1906 and the commencement of the British/German naval race, the exigencies of war produced an unprecedented demand for destroyers and escort vessels – a requirement which many of Glasgow's shipyards were soon pressed to supply. Much of the impact of this move to a war footing is discussed and illustrated in Chapters 9, 10 and 11.

In this chapter we will look at some of the perhaps less obvious consequences that the coming of the Great War brought to Glasgow, including the involvement of women in war work and defence activities. However, the huge impact that the demands of war brought to the traditional local male industries, such as shipbuilding, cannot be ignored and the photographs in this chapter include some evocative glimpses of life in the yards.

The war saw an increasing involvement of the Government in industrial

Fig. 19
Although photographed at John Brown's yard at Clydebank, and thus not strictly a Glasgow photograph, this First World War photograph of a girl bringing her father's lunch to the yard surely represents a delightful domestic scene that could have taken place in any of the city's shipyards.
(Imperial War Museum)

and social policy. The demands for war production often conflicted with established trade union practices, and by government decree, employers were allowed to 'dilute' skilled trades by employing unskilled labour in skilled jobs. Breaking complex tasks down into smaller, more easily learned components, which could be performed without a lengthy training or apprenticeship, frequently achieved this aim. There were some restrictive practices in the traditional structure of industry but the urgent needs of war production forced changes and demonstrated that alternative systems and structures were possible. Much of what had been jealously guarded as skilled work only capable of being performed by time-served men could in fact be carried out by semi-skilled workers, or even, amazingly, by women.

A key moment in this process came with the creation of the Ministry of Munitions in May 1915 and the passing of the Munitions of War Act, which introduced binding arbitration in industrial disputes and made strikes and lockouts illegal, capped profits, made the restriction of output a criminal offence and provided a legal framework for dilution. The provisions of the act, including the provision for the introduction of semi-skilled or female labour were intended to be strictly temporary:

Any departure during the war from the practice ruling in the workshops, shipyards, and other industries prior to the war, shall only be for the period of the war.

No change in practice made during the war shall be allowed to prejudice the position of the workmen in the owners' employment, or of their trade unions in regard to the resumption and maintenance after the war of any rules and customs existing prior to the war.

However clearly this was stated there still existed a considerable degree of distrust between the two sides of industry and workers were suspicious of the good faith of employers and the long-term effects of dilution. The Clyde engineering strikes of February 1915 resulted in the formation of the Clyde Workers Committee, whose members took a more aggressive line against dilution than did the official union structures. Willie Gallacher (1881–1966), later Communist MP for West Fife from 1935 to 50, then an engineering worker and leader of the Clyde Workers Committee, put the workers' argument in his memoir *Revolt on the Clyde*. Describing a meeting with the Minister of Munitions, David Lloyd George, he wrote:

The position therefore stood as follows: the Minister wanted a large influx of new labour, dilution. We had no objection to this. The only question at issue between us was: who was going to control the process – the employers or the workers?

Another 'Red Clydesider' present at this meeting, David Kirkwood, said that the issue was 'Who's going to control the factories? And I tell you ... we are.'

Lloyd George's war-time visits to Glasgow were not marked with great success. On Christmas Day 1915 he addressed a mass meeting in the city's St Andrew's Hall, where even the famed oratory of the 'Welsh Wizard' failed to win him a hearing from the assembled crowds of Clydeside workers. The Glasgow socialist periodical *Forward* edited by Tom Johnston (1882–1965) published an uncensored account of this meeting which resulted in *Forward* being suppressed under wartime emergency powers – a temporary banning which as Johnston wrote later was 'an advertisement worth thousands of pounds'.

Many of the leaders of the Clyde workers' movement were imprisoned or deported from the area. Deportation conjures up an image of Botany Bay or Devil's Island – in this case the destination was usually Edinburgh.

Despite the 'Red Clydeside' image and militancy in defence of established working practices and pay rates, there was less local evidence of anti-war sentiment than might have been expected. But John Maclean (1879–1923), a school-teacher and Marxist activist and Willie Gallacher, the 'revolutionary agitator' (his own description) who was Chair of the Clyde Workers Committee, were among the Glaswegian voices which sought to transform the industrial struggle into a more generalised political, class or anti-war campaign.

One consequence of the increase in munitions work and the influx of labour into the Glasgow area was a marked housing shortage. Although hundreds of thousands of Glasgow men had enlisted and were away from home, their families were still resident in the city and occupying the family home. The workers from elsewhere who arrived in Glasgow to take up work in defence factories sought affordable accommodation. Landlords saw this increased demand for housing as the signal to raise rents. The situation was exacerbated by the eviction of tenants for arrears of rents – an especially emotive action when the family of a serviceman was being evicted. In the spring and summer of 1915, a largely female-led movement organised an effective rent strike and refused to pay their rents in protest against these increases. At the peak of this campaign around 25,000 tenants were involved. The government intervened and introduced legislation in December 1915 to freeze Scottish rents of under £30 per annum; elsewhere the limit was £26 (and £35 in London). These restrictions applied for the duration of the war and for six months thereafter. The rent strike campaign was a very early example of the involvement of working-class Glasgow women in political activity. The pre-war suffrage campaigns were predominantly middle-class in character and, although involving a number of working-class women, were principally led by upper- and middle-class women.

The problem of drink was one that occupied the mind of Government and steps were taken to control both the strength of drink and its availability in the munitions manufacturing areas. There was indeed a serious campaign against drink during the war, with King George V setting the tone by renouncing the use of alcohol by himself and his household for the duration of the war. Although such measures, which included a prohibition on 'treating' or buying rounds, were not popular with Glasgow's drinkers, they were not the subject of organised political protest. There had always been a strong temperance strand within the tradition of socialism in Glasgow and the west of Scotland. Many of its leading figures, such as Tom Johnston, were strongly opposed to the drink trade and had campaigned for the introduction of discretionary veto polls, which would allow communities to ban licensed properties. The legislation for these had been enacted in 1913 in the Temperance (Scotland) Act but the war prevented its implementation. However in the post-war years many areas, including Johnston's own home town of Kirkintilloch, went 'dry'.

At the beginning of the war, as the scale of operations became clear and as casualty lists grew, it became apparent that the existing military and civilian hospital facilities of the country would be quite inadequate to deal with the treatment and rehabilitation of wounded servicemen evacuated from the theatres of war. All round the country offers of accommodation were made and many large private homes were converted into temporary hospitals. In Glasgow the directors of the North British Locomotive Company decided that, despite the demands of munitions production, they could make available most of their recently completed administration block in Flemington Street, Springburn, built in 1909 at a cost of £64,000. This opened for the reception of patients on Christmas Eve 1914 and closed on 21 May 1918. During the four years of its operation under the auspices of the Scottish branch of the British Red Cross Society the Springburn Hospital treated 8,211 servicemen. The building was altered to create five wards, with a total bed capacity of 400, plus ancillary accommodation. There was a resident staff of a medical superintendent and five assistants, a matron, eight sisters, seventeen nurses and thirty VADs. At the beginning of the war many young women were recruited to work as assistant nurses, ambulance drivers and cooks in Voluntary Aid Detachments. These VADs had been created in

1909 but were greatly expanded on the outbreak of war. After 1915 VADs aged over twenty-three were allowed to serve overseas, and worked in France and the Middle East. Over 38,000 VADs were recruited during the war. A similar body, the First Aid Nursing Yeomanry, was formed in 1907. Both these organisations tended to recruit young women from the middle and upper ranks of society.

Young women whose tastes and talents ran more in military than in caring channels were recruited into the Women's Volunteer Reserve, which was formed in December 1914 with Lady Castlereagh, the daughter-in-law of the 6th Marquess of Londonderry, as Colonel-in-Chief. The corps sought to enrol qualified drivers, motor-cyclists and aviators and intended to specialise in the skills of signalling, first-aid, cooking, riding and driving. The object was to create a uniformed and disciplined body of women who could, in the event of an invasion or other emergency, assist the regular forces in transport and communications work. Recruitment was open to women between eighteen and forty and a medical examination was required for entry. The Honorary Colonel of the Reserve was Evelina Haverfield, who had been a prominent militant suffragette but who like many suffragette leaders, including Christabel and Emmeline Pankhurst, threw her support behind the Government on the outbreak of war. In 1916 Evelina Haverfield went with Dr Elsie Inglis and the Scottish Women's Hospital to Serbia as head of transport. Dr Inglis, who had been a prominent Scottish suffrage campaigner before the war, turned her energies to war work and her Scottish Hospital had established a women's medical unit in France just three months after the outbreak of the war and had a 200-bed hospital running at Royaumont Abbey by 1915.

Eventually all the armed services would create women's auxiliary units. The Women's Army Auxiliary Corps – the WAACs – being first in the field in 1917, swiftly followed by the Women's Royal Naval Service – the WRNS or Wrens and the Women's Royal Air Force – the WRAF. Other opportunities for women's service developed with the Women's Land Service Corps, formed in 1917 in response to the food crisis caused by the recruitment of male farm workers for the services and German U-boat attacks on merchant shipping bringing in imported foodstuffs. A branch of the Land Service Corps, the Women's Forestry Corps, involved women in this arduous work – a far cry indeed from the accepted contemporary norms of appropriate womanly activity. By 1918 members of the voluntary Women's Police Service were on duty in the streets of Glasgow exercising a degree of moral control over the behaviour of women and girls – the conduct of women in wartime being a matter of considerable discussion and debate with frequently expressed

concerns about moral laxity and declining standards.

The realisation that women could perform many of the non-combat roles of soldiers and sailors was quite slow in dawning on the authorities. But once women had been taken on, often in fairly limited roles, it soon became apparent that they could perform much of the work of men. The Admiralty, for example, in recruiting 3,000 women in November 1917, envisaged them performing domestic duties such as cooking, cleaning or acting as mess waiters (and only accepted even this radical departure in the face of severe manpower shortages). Indeed the initial slogan for the launch of the WRNS had been: 'Free a Man for Sea Service'. However, in a short time the WRNS had doubled in number and were performing over a hundred different jobs in the Navy.

The changing role of women was of great social and political significance, even if in many cases the end of the war brought a swift return to former practices. Munitions works and engineering concerns lost no time in paying off women workers as men were demobilised and came home from the forces. The armed services rapidly shut down their female auxiliaries, although, the lesson having been learned, they were swiftly re-activated in 1939. A permanent change had however taken place in the perception of women's social, political and industrial roles and the pre-1914 world was gone for ever.

One of the most significant consequences of the Great War was the loss of a large part of an entire generation – leaving many widows and many women who would never find a husband. In both cases these women were likely to become economically and socially independent and the possibility of their continuing to be treated as dependents and second-class citizens became increasingly, if slowly, diminished. In the long run, social and political equality could not be denied to women and the gradual extension of the franchise was one manifestation of the change that the war had brought. Single women ratepayers had had the vote in municipal elections from 1869 and the 1918 Representation of the People Act gave the vote to all women over thirty. In 1928 women were eventually given the vote on the same terms as men – that is at the age of twenty-one.

Another very obvious and very public manifestation of the effects of the war was the dedication of memorials to commemorate the huge loss of life suffered by the city over the four years. The most public and most central expression of this was the Cenotaph in George Square, unveiled on 30 May 1924 by Earl Haig. As Lord Provost Montgomery said on this occasion:

It would never be possible to secure a definite figure as to the number of those belonging to the city who served in the war ... and it would be equally impossible ever to know the precise number of those who fell and gave their lives for the great cause, they had on record on their Roll of Honour close upon 20,000 names.

Other memorials in the city include plaques in Glasgow Cathedral marking the sacrifice of members of the three 'Pals' battalions of the Highland Light Infantry.

Fig. 20
A musical interlude for some off-duty nurses, VADs and a sister enjoying the amenities of the nurse's rest room at Springburn Hospital.
(Mitchell Library: North British Locomotive Collection)

GLASGOW: A CITY AT WAR

Fig. 21 (top)

This striking view of the Fairfield shipbuilding yard at Govan on the south bank of the Clyde, taken during the First World War gives a vivid impression of the activity of the yard and the mixture of modern cranes and traditional scaffolding used in the construction. Note the large merchant vessel lying at Meadowside Quay on the north bank of the river, painted in war-time dazzle camouflage.
(Imperial War Museum)

Fig. 22 (below)

Victoria Ward at Springburn Red Cross Hospital. The large and well-lit spaces of the North British Locomotive Company's Administration building were well suited to rapid conversion into large wards, of a sort which might have been recognised by Florence Nightingale. The somewhat spartan surroundings and fairly intensively packed rows of beds probably conformed to the normal standards for military and civilian hospitals at this time.
(Mitchell Library: North British Locomotive Collection)

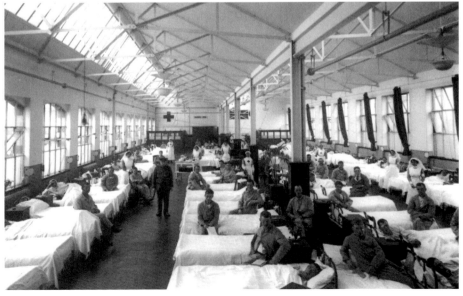

Fig. 23 (below)
A quiet afternoon for some convalescent patients enjoying the facilities of a dayroom at Springburn Red Cross Hospital. A waist-coated civilian has found his way in and is watching the skills being displayed at the billiard table. Sir Frederick Milner, who inspected Springburn Hospital on behalf of King George V, wrote in February 1916: 'I was more charmed with Springburn than ever, and give it first prize of all the hospitals I have seen. It is quite perfect, and the men seem so happy and contented.'
*(Mitchell Library:
North British Locomotive
Collection)*

Fig. 24

Field Marshall French (1852–1925) was commander in chief of the British Expeditionary Force sent to France in 1914. His direction of the British forces was less than successful and his relationship with the French commanders was strained. In December 1915 he resigned command, was created a viscount, and appointed as commander in chief of Home Forces in 1916. This role, with responsibility for training and for defence of the UK against air attack, proved to be more successful for French. In this capacity he came to Glasgow on 26 June 1917 to inspect a parade of volunteers at Fleshers' Haugh, Glasgow Green. Four battalions of the Glasgow Volunteer Regiment were on parade, together with the Volunteer Motor Corps, and, as our photograph shows, the Women's Volunteer Reserve. Ten officers and 206 other ranks of this unit paraded for Lord French's inspection under their commanding officer Major Lander. *(Imperial War Museum)*

Fig. 25

Although women workers were increasingly used in the manufacturing industry during the First World War, they were frequently trained to perform only a limited number of functions, with manufacturing processes being broken down into discrete elements which could be learned swiftly and efficiently. This photograph of women workers in the engraving department of Barr & Stroud shows a single male employee. Very often, even in overwhelmingly female departments, the supervisory staff and tool-setters were male. *(Thales Optronics)*

Fig. 26

It was not only private enterprise that saw a great increase in the number of women workers and in the range of work they undertook. Public bodies also had to adapt to the male labour shortage caused by the vast expansion in the armed forces. The Glasgow City Council had to recruit women to work as tramway conductors and drivers (see photograph in Chapter 8) as a result of the severe staff shortages caused by the great success of the recruitment campaign to raise a Tramways Battalion of the Highland Light Infantry. The Corporation's Electrical Department – a municipally owned electricity supply company created in 1892 – took on women workers for its stores section at Port Dundas in February 1916. The photograph shows some of these female employees, who were able to earn the fairly substantial pay of £1.16s.5d (including bonus) for a 54-hour week. *(Imperial War Museum)*

Fig. 27
The North British Locomotive Company was largely turned over to munitions work and very large numbers of women workers were engaged on shell production. This photograph shows women munitions workers filleting copper bands for 9.2-inch and 8-inch shells at the Hydepark Works. *(Gallacher Collection, Glasgow Caledonian University)*

[4]

THE FEAR OF THE BOMBER

The idea that wars were fought by professional armies in distant lands and did not impinge on the everyday life of the civilian population was a peculiarly British one – and a peculiarly time-specific one created by this island's substantial lack of armed conflict on its soil in the eighteenth and nineteenth centuries. The long wars with France, the war with the infant United States, the Crimean War and the many wars of Empire all were fought by the Navy or the Army, but were conveniently insulated from the day-to-day experience of the home population.

This was not how most of the world knew war. It was not even how the people of these islands had traditionally known war.

The people of the Lothians and the Borders who found their homes destroyed, their crops burned, their cattle slaughtered, their churches desecrated by invading English armies could testify to that. As could the people of northern England, ravaged in their turn by invading Scottish armies.

The Europe of the Hundred Years War even evolved a technical term for this systematic raiding and destruction of the economic potential of the lands of the enemy – *chevauchée*.

But for over two centuries war had been distanced from the experience of the civilian population of Britain. Obviously the deaths of soldiers and sailors, economic disruption, conscription and so forth had their impact, but eighteenth- and nineteenth-century war was, for most of the population, something to read about in the papers. Jane Austen (1775–1817) lived her adult life and wrote her novels while the long war with Revolutionary and Napoleonic France was going on and, while soldiers and sailors appear in her works (and Austen's brother was a naval officer), the ordered life of English society is seemingly little affected by the life and death struggle on the high seas, in the Peninsula and in colonies around the globe.

The First World War changed all that for the British people, if only to a limited extent. German warships bombarded east coast towns, Zeppelin airships carried out fifty-one raids on Britain, while German aeroplanes

Fig. 28

Glasgow, like other strategically important sites, was soon ringed with anti-aircraft artillery sites. The number of guns deployed grew rapidly as the threat from the German air force increased and as they were able to operate from air bases in Holland, France, Denmark and Norway – those increasing their range and bringing even more of the United Kingdom into the endangered area. By September 1940 there were thirty-four heavy anti-aircraft guns deployed in the Clyde area under the command of the 3rd Anti-Aircraft Division. These guns were of 3-inch, 3.7-inch and 4.5-inch calibre with the 3.7-inch gun the most common. Our photograph shows a typical anti-aircraft emplacement with the gun at top left. In the foreground is a height-finder for directing the gunfire. *(The Daily Record)*

carried out fifty-two raids. In the course of these two sets of raids 4,820 people were killed and injured. These were, inevitably, terror attacks. A military target might have been identified but the technology available meant that collateral civilian deaths were inevitable. Scotland did not escape these raids – two German naval Zeppelins bombed Edinburgh on the night of 2 April 1916. Thirteen people died and twenty-four were injured in this attack.

The experience of attacks on the civilian population in the First World War led to the establishment in 1924 by the British Cabinet's Committee of Imperial Defence of a sub-committee on Air Raid Precautions. The largely confidential work of this sub-committee did not impinge greatly on public consciousness and implementation of its proposals was inhibited by the application of the 'Ten Year Rule': a British Government doctrine that no major war was likely, or should be budgeted for, in a rolling period of ten years, a funding restraint which was only removed in November 1933.

The years between the two world wars were ones in which the technology of aviation developed rapidly – aircraft became larger, faster, capable of flying further and carrying greater loads. The bomber aircraft became seen as the ultimate weapon. All the major powers developed such aircraft and used them – the British in enforcing their mandate in Iraq used airpower to quell unrest, the Italians bombed and gassed in Abyssinia and the German Condor Legion fighting in the Spanish Civil War attacked civilian targets – most notoriously the Basque and Republican town of Guernica, which was bombed and virtually destroyed in April 1937.

All of this contributed to a deep official and popular concern about the threat and likely horrors of air attack in a future war. The Committee of Imperial Defence in 1937 produced an estimate that in a future war an initial air campaign against London might last for sixty days and kill 600,000 people. The belief that 'the bomber will always get through', articulated by Stanley Baldwin, then Lord President of the Council in Ramsay MacDonald's National Government, in a speech in the House of Commons in November 1932, took hold and a very serious concern that air attack – possibly including gas attack – would destroy the nation's capacity to fight and to survive became widespread and became the subject of much debate and concern. It even became the theme of popular fiction – as for example in Nevil Shute's 1939 novel *What Happened to the Corbetts?*

While much of the military planning of the mid-1930s was centred on London – an enormous, easily reached and easily attacked target – nationwide civil defence measures – or Air Raid Precautions (ARPs) – were put in hand from 1935 onwards. The scale of these measures increased as the decade wore on and the threat from Germany became ever clearer. At the time of the Munich crisis in September 1938 sandbags appeared round public buildings, trenches were dug in public parks as improvised air-raid shelters and 35 million respirators were distributed to the civilian population. Munich bought time, which was put to effective use to develop an elaborate system of defence measures against the threat of the bomber. By the time of the Munich crisis half a million citizens had volunteered for ARP duties but in the next few months this number was doubled.

In March 1939 gas mask cases were distributed and in the same month large-scale ARP exercises were carried out throughout the country to test sirens, blackout arrangements, and the use of searchlights.

In February 1939 Glasgow City Council was asked to identify the number of steel air-raid shelters that would be needed – these were what came to be known as Anderson shelters, after Sir John Anderson, the cabinet minister responsible for civil defence matters. These shelters were supplied free to families with an income of less that £250 per year – a figure that was increased by £50 for each child under school age. The galvanised corrugated steel shelters could be assembled by two people without any special skills and were designed to be partially sunk in back gardens, the excavated earth being piled up to provide extra protection against blast and splinters.

Of course most Glasgow residents did not live in houses with back (or front) gardens and at the beginning of the war steel struts were provided to reinforce tenement closes and turn them, with the assistance of sand-bagged baffle walls at the entrance, into improvised air-raid shelters.

The fear of the bomber and the growing realisation that war was inevitable produced a variety of responses, some practical, some less so. The Glasgow and West of Scotland College of Domestic Science discovered an old and disused sewage tunnel under its premises, and with a thorough cleaning, liberal application of whitewash and the provision of chairs, converted it into an air-raid shelter. Councillor Gordon Cochrane, a Progressive (i.e. Conservative) member of the City Council proposed a massive extension of the city's subway system to serve such distant suburbs as Knightswood and Mosspark. Noting that the tunnelling costs would be £1 million per mile he observed that apart from solving Glasgow's transport problems the tunnels would provide first rate air-raid shelters.

After the outbreak of war, in November 1939, the Glasgow press reported that work had started on two tunnel shelters – one created in Carron Street, Springburn, by excavation of the hillside, and one created from a railway tunnel near the Gallowgate.

Glaswegians were able to inspect a pill-box type concrete air-raid shelter which was erected in the city's Central Station in March 1939. This shelter was claimed to be strong enough to withstand the debris from the collapse of a three-storey building. Speaking after the opening of this demonstration shelter Lord Provost Patrick Dollan said that a complete system of public air-raid shelters in Glasgow could cost £12 million – and even a modified scheme might cost £3 million. The concrete shelter was an option for families who would not receive the free Anderson shelter, could be erected immediately by any builder and could serve as a store room or garden shed in peace-time.

Public and political responses to these measures varied widely. Many on the Left of politics were hostile to the concept of military or civil preparedness, feeling that such measures made war more, not less, likely.

The Scottish Socialist Party, at a conference in Glasgow in April 1939, condemned the rumoured introduction of conscription. One Bo'ness delegate to the conference also condemned Lord Provost Dollan for his support for munitions factories in Glasgow:

> … the most vulnerable point in any community is that part which contains a munition factory. It is the focal point and the target which will be aimed at by enemy 'planes. It is a direct incentive and inducement to enemy bombers to pay a visit to Glasgow in order to destroy the source of supply of the Government bombing 'planes.

Perhaps the most significant munitions factory to be developed in Glasgow was the Rolls Royce aero-engine plant at Hillington, work on which commenced in May 1939; it was designed to become the largest aero-engine factory in the world – being six times larger than Rolls Royce's Crewe works.

Members of the British Communist Party had to perform a swift *volte-face* in August 1939 when the Nazi–Soviet Pact was signed and Hitler's Germany suddenly became a respected partner of the Soviet Union – a *volte-face* which had to be repeated, in reverse, when Hitler invaded the Soviet Union in June 1941.

Glasgow's Lord Provost Patrick Dollan, although on the Left of politics, was an enthusiastic advocate of civil defence and military preparedness. In February 1939 he noted with concern the poor response of the city's municipal employees to the call for ARP volunteers – he told a meeting of their union that not more than one in ten of them had volunteered and that this had significantly contributed to the huge shortfall in the city's ARP numbers. Forty thousand volunteers were needed and so far only 13,200 had come forward, 60 per cent of them drawn from private sector employment. However, during 1939 recruitment picked up and at the end of April Lord

Provost Dollan, speaking before a recruitment rally at Hampden Park, identified just 8,000 vacancies in National Service organisations and 6,000 in Territorial Army units. The shortfall in the Territorial Army had been caused by the order that all TA units should double their strength – or as it was put in military terms, 'recruit the second line'.

Dollan had to return to the civil defence recruitment problem again in May when he pointed out in a speech that twelve of Glasgow's thirty-eight wards had still not reached their target for civil defence volunteers. He named the Camphill, Pollokshields, Pollokshaws area in the south of the city as being short of 600 air-raid wardens.

Councillor Jean Roberts, who would become the city's first female Lord Provost in 1960, but was then the convener of the Glasgow Women's ARP Committee, authorised the city's Medical Officer of Health to organise classes for the instruction of women in first aid.

Recruiting for the various elements of the Air Raid Precautions system went on apace in 1939 with efforts being made to bring up to strength various components of the ARP system such as the Auxiliary Fire Service. This was a force designed to augment the regular fire brigades in dealing with fires caused by bombing and consisted of a warden service, rescue and demolition parties, first aid parties to work in bombed areas, staff for first aid and casualty clearing posts, and ambulance drivers and attendants.

The Auxiliary Fire Service in Glasgow would grow to eventually staff thirty-five stations across the city, many of them established in school premises. The AFS Station at Bankhead School was bombed on the night of 13 March 1941 and twenty-one lives were lost.

In March 1939 it was reported that 5,000 employees of the Post Office in Glasgow had received training in anti-gas measures.

Going on in parallel with these civilian measures were steps to improve the air defences of the country. Glasgow – and the economically vital Clyde area – was beyond range of German aircraft based in Germany (although considerably more at risk if German forces moved into the Low Countries or France) and consequently was not a priority area for fighter aircraft – most of which were concentrated on the south coast of England – or for the rapidly developing radar network.

The Observer Corps, a volunteer body, had been established in 1925 and charged with reporting on the movement of aircraft across those areas of the country which were considered to be open to attack (it was granted the title Royal Observer Corps in April 1941). By 1940 the radar chain and the Observer Corps network had embraced the Glasgow and Clyde area. The Observer Corps volunteers, male and female, worked four-hour shifts around the clock, keeping up a non-stop surveillance. Even after the main German air attacks had ceased there was still the risk of surprise raids. While radar could detect distant aircraft, the work of the Observer Corps in identifying type, height, speed and direction and passing this information on to the RAF controllers would prove to be vital.

Other steps were taken within a generally quickening mood of re-armament and realisation of the likelihood of war – 602 City of Glasgow Squadron of the Auxiliary Air Force was brought to combat readiness by re-equipping it with Hawker Hectors – a bi-plane used specifically for army co-operation work. Shortly after this its status was again raised by becoming the first Auxiliary Air Force Squadron to be equipped with Spitfire fighters in April 1939, ahead of many regular RAF squadrons. A Royal Air Force Volunteer Reserve had been created in 1936.

The air threat was also recognised by the conversion of a number of Territorial Army infantry battalions into anti-aircraft artillery units late in 1938.

The year 1939 saw the arrival of searchlights and barrage balloons in Glasgow. Three RAF Squadrons – Nos. 945, 946 and 947 – recruited volunteers in and around the Glasgow area and the first hundred volunteers to join were sworn in by Lord Provost Dollan, in his capacity as Lord Lieutenant of the County of the City of Glasgow, in March 1939. Dollan praised the democratic nature of the unit:

> For the first time in Glasgow it will be made possible for men who join as privates in the balloon barrage squadrons to rise from the ranks by merit. No question of means will deprive any of you from promotion from the ranks. You are entitled to be called the defenders of Clydeside.

Dollan's speech gives a valuable insight into attitudes to the bomber threat. He said that when the squadrons were fully operative it would be almost impossible for enemy aircraft to spray gas on the city, to indulge in low-flight attacks, and to succeed in great attacks on military and industrial objectives. The balloon barrages would compel enemy aircraft to fly at a great height. He added:

> In fact with the balloon barrage squadrons and anti-aircraft units we can practically make Glasgow immune from serious attack from the air, and that is very important, because Glasgow in time of war will be the chief industrial centre of Great Britain.

Dollan's appreciation of the city's strategic role, if perhaps slightly overstated, reflected Glasgow's relative geographical isolation from enemy bomber bases. The city and its region were indeed to be a key industrial centre and a key centre for shipping, military supplies and troop movements as will be seen in Chapter 12. However, even when the balloon barrage was fully developed – and in July 1940 there were 120 barrage balloons manned by the three squadrons in the Glasgow/Renfrew area – this did not make Glasgow immune from aerial attack (see Chapter 5).

One particular fear arising from the bomber threat was the loss of lives among children. In January 1939 the Government published its plans for the evacuation of civilians from the centres of population thought to be most under threat of attack. Local authorities were instructed to conduct a census of spare accommodation in safer areas. Priority in the evacuation was to be given to children and, where possible, children were to be moved in school groups accompanied by teachers and other adult helpers. Children under school age were to be accompanied by their mothers or other persons who were responsible for looking after them. Most evacuated children were to be billeted in private houses, although in February 1939 the government announced a £1 million programme to build school camps, which would be used to take groups of city children to the country in peace-time but which could also serve as evacuation centres in war.

Plans were firmed up in May when powers were taken in the Civil Defence Bill for the compulsory requisitioning of accommodation for evacuees from vulnerable areas; local authorities were given billeting powers early in August.

The elaborate plans made for the evacuation of 190,000 people from Glasgow which had been drawn up in the last months and weeks of peace were put into effect on 1 September – two days before the declaration of war.

Seventy thousand school children, pre-school children, mothers and helpers were scheduled for evacuation on 1st September and the fifty-six schools chosen for this initial evacuation were in the most congested and thickly populated areas of the city. Another fifty-seven schools were to be evacuated on 2 September and seventy-three to be cleared on Sunday 3 September. Children from Glasgow and Clydebank were sent to Aberdeenshire, Argyll, Bute, Dumfries, Dumbartonshire, Kinross-shire, Kirkcudbrightshire, Lanarkshire, Perthshire, Renfrewshire, Stirlingshire and Wigtownshire.

Fig. 29
Apart from domestic and public shelters, industrial concerns also had to build their own shelters to provide cover for workers during air-raids. These shelters were, naturally, better organised than 'free for all' public shelters and this illustration shows a ticket allocating a space in a designated shelter and the route that had to be taken to reach safety. *(Kevin Morrison Collection, Glasgow Caledonian University)*

As soon as Warning Siren sounds proceed immediately to SHELTER No. 4

ROUTE :— Proceed from Kilblain Street Exit via Nicholson Street to Yard behind New Shop.

GLASGOW: A CITY AT WAR

The city children found themselves in accommodation ranging from farm-workers' cottages to baronial halls. The *Glasgow Herald's* correspondents found 'an almost unanimous determination amongst householders in these districts to make their youthful charges as happy and comfortable as possible'. Schools in the reception areas were pressed into service as receiving depots from where the evacuated children could be allocated to houses in the neighbourhood.

As an initial response to the threat of air attack all day schools in Glasgow and other evacuation areas were closed, as were cinemas, theatres and football grounds. These latter closures were soon rescinded as being too damaging to public morale. There should, theoretically, have been no need for schools to be open in Glasgow as all school-age children were to be evacuated. However, on 4th September it was reported that some 30,000 of the projected 190,000 evacuees had failed to report and there was later an unofficial drift back from the countryside to the city. So many children had never left the city, or had returned to it, that in October a group of Govan mothers called on the Lord Provost at the City Chambers to demand the immediate re-opening of city schools, claiming that children were running wild and becoming demoralised owing to the lack of educational discipline.

Fig. 30

An essential part of the defence against night bombing attacks was the searchlight. Glasgow had enjoyed a spectacular pre-war demonstration of searchlight operations when in April 1939 men of the 57th Searchlight Regiment deployed two projectors in George Square and showed how aircraft could be picked up and held in the beam. As a newspaper report said 'the way the planes were held once found gripped the attention of a large crowd'. This dramatic photograph from late 1939 shows a searchlight crew standing-to at dusk 'somewhere in Scotland'. *(The Daily Record)*

Fig. 31

The barrage balloon formed a key element in the defence against the bomber and was intended to deter low-flying precision bombing attacks. This photograph shows a naval-manned barrage balloon at a Clydeside location. The difficulties of controlling the balloon are demonstrated by the two ratings on the right of the picture who have been lifted off their feet by the gas-filled balloon. *(Imperial War Museum)*

Fig. 32

Although the human costs of the evacuation, with children being separated from their parents and having to adjust to a new way of life, should not be underestimated, many children found the evacuation an exciting adventure. This group of children have clearly found a very congenial environment in *Duneira*, a large villa in Rhu, on the Gareloch, some 25 miles from Glasgow. They are enjoying a splendid selection of books, toys and comics, including the *Dandy* and one retelling the adventures of Tarzan. The quiet backwater of the Gareloch was very soon to become a major strategic centre, with flying-boats being based at Rhu and a huge military port being created a couple of miles further up the loch at Shandon. *(The Daily Record)*

Fig. 33

The planned evacuation of children from target areas such as Glasgow was a vital part of contingency planning before the war began and it is a credit to the planners that, in general, the system worked well. This photograph shows a cheerful group of Glasgow school-children and their teacher going off to a government evacuation camp at Abington, Lanarkshire. The box each child is carrying around their shoulders or over their neck is their gas-mask container.

(The Daily Record)

Fig. 34

Air-raid shelters took many forms – the Anderson shelter in the back garden, the reinforced close-mouth, the underground tunnel, the brick and concrete shelter built above ground. This 1940 photograph shows one of the last mentioned, in George Square, Glasgow, with a workman checking the door. Note the white paint defining the edges of the building and the door – an aid to visibility in black-out conditions. Note also the posters on the shelter wall. The war-time population was regularly exhorted by posters to avoid waste or careless talk ('Be Like Dad, Keep Mum!' was a favourite slogan), to dig for victory and to save for victory. The extreme right-hand poster is advertising National War Bonds.
(*The Daily Record*)

[5]

TERROR FROM THE SKY

T he twentieth century was the one that first saw aerial combat and in which the skies first became a medium of destruction to industrial, and even more horrifically to civilian, targets. The Scottish novelist, Neil Munro, joined H.G. Wells and other fiction writers in imagining this kind of futuristic scenario. In a piece written for the *Evening News* on 16 November 1908 Munro visualises the pulverising effect of an assault by a German 'airship fleet' upon the Clyde:

> The German aerial fleet was first observed in a wedge-shape formation sailing rapidly from the east at half-past seven – less than two hours after it had left the Rosyth naval base in ruins, and blown the Forth Bridge into fragments ... the airships darted in two parallel lines down the river banks and threw bombs into all the shipbuilding yards.

Munro's pessimistic vision of the future concentrates on the vulnerability of industrial targets – he describes the Clyde as the 'workshop river'. In a sense, though, he is not pessimistic enough, as civilian casualties in the second great conflict of the century were to show. The Second World War produced casualties in thousands on Clydeside. The Great War had seen some aerial action in Scotland – Edinburgh had been on the receiving end of a Zeppelin raid – but Glasgow had no such experience. Airships, and in particular the German Zeppelins, were believed at the time Munro was writing to be the future of offensive operations in the air – although Munro's comic character, Erchie, was among the first to spot the vulnerability of the machines he described as being like a 'Trades' Hoose cigar'.

For Glasgow, the story in the Second World War was indeed very different. The air-raids were much more concentrated attacks, even if only over a relatively short period. As shown in Chapter 4, the fear of death delivered from the air had grown in the years since the last war. The destruction of cities like Guernica, and other Fascist bombing atrocities in the Spanish Civil War, were still fresh in people's minds. Most military theorists argued that the next war

Fig. 35
This fascinating aerial reconnaissance photograph shows that Goering's Luftwaffe were in possession of good intelligence about industrial targets in the area of the Glasgow docks and shipyards. Taken in October 1939, it lists the outlined target areas, including: Meadowside Quay; Fairfield's and Harland and Wolff's shipyards; Queen's and Prince's Dock; Clyde Navigation Trust drydocks.
(Imperial War Museum)

GLASGOW: A CITY AT WAR

would be won quickly and decisively by a sudden or 'lightning' onslaught – an intense aerial bombardment of cities and their civilian populations, paralysing their communications and industrial bases. The Germans would bomb Britain for up to sixty days following the declaration of war, it was believed. Six hundred thousand people would be killed and double that number injured. Poison gas would probably be used (hence the carrying of gas masks). It was an article of faith that 'the bomber will always get through'.

For Glasgow and Clydeside as a whole the spring of 1941 was the time when any remaining feeling that this was simply to be a 'phoney war' was abandoned. For London, Coventry, Liverpool and elsewhere south of the Border, the harsh reality of aerial warfare had come earlier. The interesting evidence of the unique 'Mass Observation' project – which recorded the reactions of a wide cross-section of people at war – was that any notion of 'morale' under bombing attacks had to take account of the actual local circumstances. Morale, it seemed, was not only influenced by the intensity of a raid and the scale and nature of the damage sustained; it was also noted that '... people's ability to withstand attack declined as the raids increased in frequency, or threatened to do so'. Mass Observation concluded that such 'repetitive' bombing: 'was much the hardest type of attack to get used to ... it is very doubtful if people can condition themselves to more than three nights of intensive attack in a week'.

The initial impression left by the German attacks on Poland and elsewhere in mainland Europe seemed to confirm this, but by the time of the Clydeside raids, everyone had seen London's resilience in the face of the bombing. The capital could 'take it'. From that evidence it seemed that the bombing of Britain was not going to be a 'lightning war', or 'blitzkrieg', as it was termed in German, as had happened in Poland and elsewhere. It was to be much more of a war of attrition, but nevertheless the name stuck and 'blitz' became everyone's word for the bombing raids. Angus Calder wrote in *The Myth of the Blitz*:

> As heavy bombing of London began in the late summer, the word 'blitz' became almost overnight a British colloquialism for an air-raid. But from the first it suggested more than that. It was instantaneously and spontaneously 'mythologised'.

Now it was time for the people of Glasgow to participate in the myth. Just as Londoners' resilience in the face of massive bombing was believed to be evidence of an inexhaustible ability to 'take it', so Clydesiders were now to be suddenly tested in the heat of battle. Glaswegians, for the first time in many centuries, found themselves, in a sense, in the front line, but a front line in which they personally had no opportunity for self-defence or for retaliation. There was heroism, just as in London, but equally there was scepticism and anger. Churchill was booed in Scotland as he had been in the southern capital. Dr I.M.M. MacPhail, historian of the Clydebank Blitz and himself a veteran of bomb disposal units reminds us that the blitz was not simply a case of instantaneous immolation or survival:

> There were others whose deaths resulted at an interval of months or, in some cases, years from the effects of the 'blitz' and its aftermath. And indeed, even today … the scars and wounds, physical, mental and spiritual, are still to be found in the persons who lived through the 'Blitz'.

The first bombs on Glasgow fell on 19 July 1940 on Blawarthill Street, Yoker, followed soon after by others on the stadium of Benburb Junior Football Club in Craigton. On September 18 at 2.40 a.m. a large bomb was dropped on the cruiser HMS *Sussex* and there were other attacks by lone raiders for the remainder of 1940 and early 1941.

What followed in the spring of 1941 was on a different scale altogether. The first 200-bomber raid of the war was about to be unleashed on a Scottish target. The attacking German bombers that formed part of the Luftwaffe's Third Air Fleet took off from their airfields in west France as evening fell on 13 March, 1941. As they came in over the North Sea, the sirens wailed as it became clear that the 'targets for tonight' included Clydeside. This was the way that the full force of aerial war came to the towns along the river.

The attacking German aircraft on those nights carried a payload of flares and three main types of bomb: incendiaries, which set targets ablaze and acted as a beacon to following planes; high explosive (HE) bombs; and parachute mines (sometimes wrongly called landmines), which were designed to explode close to the ground, thus providing a great deal of lateral blast.

The bombing raids on the moonlit nights of 13 and 14 March (such conditions were dubbed a 'bomber's moon', because the raiders were able to find their way with ease to the target) tend to be remembered as the Clydebank Blitz. This is because of the tremendous impact on that burgh, even though as many bombs fell on the same nights on Glasgow, and there were approximately as many casualties. In total, more than 1,200 people were killed and more than 1,000 seriously injured over the two nights of bombing, although as the following table shows, it is probable that the Germans had targeted the shipyards and factories rather than people's homes.

Luftwaffe, Third Air Fleet, West France attack on Glasgow and Clydeside, 14 to 15 March 1941 (Statistics from German sources)

TIME	UNIT	TYPE	NO.	ALTITUDE (METRES)	BOMBS AND TARGETS
9.30–10.15	I. K.G. 27	He 111	7	2,5000–3,200	14 250k; 7 500k; 2,016 IB – target unspecified
9.45–9.55	III. K.G. 51	Ju 88	3	1,600–3,600	3 250k; 3 500k – east of river; harbour area
9.45–10.30	II. K.G. 76	Ju 88	14	1,500–3,500	140 50k; 56 250k; 3 500k – oil tanks
10.05–10.45	II. K.G. 27	He 111	13	3,000–4,000	North-west sector of target area 'a' – oil depot
10.07–10.35	I.K.G. 27	He 111	6	2,000–3,900	6 250k; 4 250k (DA); 6 500k – target unspecified
10.08	I. K.G. 51	Ju 88	1	3,000	1 250k; 1 500k (DA) – Rolls-Royce Works, Hillington
10.14	II. K.G. 51	Ju 88	1	3,200	1 250k; 1 500k – Rolls-Royce Works, Hillington
10.15–10.46	K.G. 77	Ju 88	10	3,000–3,300	20 50k; 22 250k; 6 250k (DA) – target unspecified
10.15–11.00	K. Gr. 100	He 111	7	3,000–3,800	14 250k; 3,024 IB – target I
10.20–11.33	III. K.G. 1	Ju 88	6	3,000–3,500	20 250k; 3 250k (DA); 1 500k – target area 'b'
10.23–11.40	I. K.G. 1	He 111	12	2,500–3,500	450k; 1 500k; 13,104 IB target unspecified
10.30–11.10	I. K.G. 55	He 111	9	2,000–2,500	15 250k; 8 500k; 2,160 IB – Rolls-Royce Works, Hillington; Princes' and Kingston Docks
10.40–11.10	II. K.G. 55	He 111	8	2,000–3,000	24 250k; 9 500k; 576 IB target unspecified
10.50–11.05	K. Gr. 806	He 111	10	2,000–3,500	40 250k – Rolls-Royce Works, Hillington
11.21–01.50	III. K.G. 6	He 111	5	3,100–3,500	5 500k; 2,880 IB – target unspecified

Abbreviations:

DA – delayed action; He – Heinkel; IB – incendiary bomb; Ju – Junkers; k – kilogram; K.G. – Kampgeschwader (Bomber squadron); K. Gr. – Kampfgruppe (Bomber group)

What were the aircraft that brought modern aerial warfare to Scotland's cities and towns? There were two main types. The Junkers 88 was among the most successful of all Second World War German bombers and remained in production in many different forms throughout the period of hostilities. The other type of aircraft employed in the German raids was the Heinkel E111. The latter was the first of the attackers participating in the March raids, and they were carrying a payload of high explosive (HE) bombs as well as flares and incendiaries as they followed the radio navigation beam. They were closely followed by other waves of Heinkels and Junkers 88s (also twin-engined bombers capable of being adapted to a fighter role).

Bombing was an inexact science compared to what it would become later in the war and, although there was a 'pathfinder' unit among the enemy planes, some of the German aircraft dropped their bombs indiscriminately and wide of target. The industrial damage was not excessive – this despite the auspicious visibility. MacPhail described the first evening of the March raids:

> … rivers and railways showed clearly to aircraft 12,000 feet above. According to the secret and confidential report from the Luftwaffe Headquarters next day, conditions were favourable to the attacking aircraft both in regard to weather and visibility; not only could the target areas be clearly identified but, it was claimed, the crews could distinguish the craters made by the bombs. In the report it was stated that 'from 22.30 hours to 06.47 hours (21.30 to 05.47 by British time) 236 bombers attacked along the length of the River Clyde with about 272 tons of high explosive bombs and 1,650 incendiary containers'.

As has already been noted, the bombing of Glasgow and the other towns on the banks of the Clyde is remembered more for the destruction of houses and death and injury of civilians than for damage to industrial or military targets. One famous instance of the latter was the aforementioned attack on the 10,000-ton cruiser HMS *Sussex* in September 1940 at Yorkhill Quay. A 250-lb bomb went through the deck, penetrated the engine room and threatened to set off an even more massive explosion in the ship's magazine. Fire crews, including those on the Govan ferry, pressed into service as a fire tender, managed eventually to flood the magazine and avoid calamity. The area around the dock, with many tenement properties accommodating about 2,000 people, was evacuated as a precaution – Yorkhill Children's Hospital was also partially cleared of its young patients.

In view of the previously mentioned conclusions of Mass Observation

GLASGOW: A CITY AT WAR

about the demoralising effects of 'repetitive' bombing, it was fortunate for Glasgow and Clydeside that the two main spells of intense bombing which affected them were weeks apart – in March and in May (when Greenock was the principal target) of 1941. So neither of these blitzes exceeded Mass Observation's three-nights-a-week figure, in contrast to several unfortunate cities in the south.

The Ministry of Information had been concerned that Glasgow's record of political unrest, reaching back to the First World War, might lead to a quasi-revolutionary situation, under the destabilising influence of heavy bombing. However, when the March raids began a different picture emerged.

The Mass Observation reports were filed at the time of these traumatic events but remained unpublished until after the war. Something of the same impartiality or objectivity can be found in another source, also not made public until the post-war years, and clearly not subject to censorship or other interference. This source was provided by the Home Intelligence reports of the Ministry of Information, and, in the case of Glasgow and Clydeside, the reports spoke of 'remarkably little grumbling' and detected a 'striking similarity' to the response and morale of London's East Enders in the face of their blitz. Engineering apprentices volunteered to suspend the strike that was going on at the time of the raids and to assist in clearing up bomb damage. In the city of Glasgow as a whole, Home Intelligence was aware of 'a sense of relief at having been able to stand up to the ordeal [of intensive bombing]'. The reports also detected 'a new feeling of partnership with the English blitzed cities'.

The foregoing is not to minimise the impact of the March blitz. 'Kept hush-hush' at first, the figures reluctantly released afterwards suggested over 1,000 killed and more than 1,600 seriously injured. Newspapers in general began by emphasising good morale – perhaps fed by information from official sources (a euphemism for propaganda) in reports under such headlines as:

FAILURE OF TERROR TACTICS

Anti-aircraft guns roared into action last night when Nazi raiders visited a central district of Scotland. The raiders were given a hot reception, and pinpoint flashes of bursting shells sparkled in the sky, the salvoes seeming to come from all sides of the area.

This was war viewed as spectacle and there was plenty of the same. Next the report turned to matters of morale:

In every district the raid was met by cold courage and sound organisation. The experience of the previous night (Thursday 13 March) had burnished the already smooth efficiency of all branches of ARP services. No sooner had the call to action come than fire-fighters, wardens, demolition squads and a host of other voluntary workers were at their posts. Mobile canteens appeared in many streets and hospitality was immediately made ready – for the bitter experience of the previous night had shown that the biggest targets of the Nazi airmen were the homes of the people.

Gradually a less optimistic view began to appear in accounts of the March raids. In the early days following the bombing a female columnist in the *Glasgow Herald* wrote a piece that in its title 'Clydebuilt', seemed to have a morale-boosting intent, but then developed a harder, more realistic edge:

We would say at once in all sincerity that this is not an 'upkeep of morale' article, briskly bright and deprecating the havoc that has come to so many … We have walked along those devastated streets, crunching all the time over littered glass speedily being swept into the gutters. We were now seeing for the first time among our own people what had happened elsewhere. These were the same as we had seen in pictures from Spain, from Finland, from Poland.

Another such dash of realism could be detected when the District Commissioner for Civil Defence, Sir Steven Bilsland, made an appeal for assistance in billeting families who had lost their homes in the blitz. Concealed in what was mainly a hymn in praise of the voluntary element and individuals' heroism was a note of uncertainty about the area's readiness for aerial bombardment: 'The success of [the billeting] depends on the spirit of co-operation among those who have been more fortunate, whose assistance will be necessary to complete it.'

Even the much-needed rescue squads were sometimes thought unsatisfactory, because levels of payment to the part-time squads was contested. Their dedication was not in question, however, as was demonstrated when one householder was rescued from a bombed property after being buried for eight days. The workers and other rescuers, as well as those who cared for the victims of the aerial onslaught, benefited from the kind of service provided by the WRVS and similar groups. Within days the press put out appeals for more mobile canteens. One of these havens of comfort had served something like 3,000 'cuppas' in three or four days. Another lesson learned in the March blitz was to try to make it harder for the German raiders to find their targets – smoke burners were located close to the river to create and lay down an artificial haze. The pattern favoured by the German raiders was to drop flares and incendiaries so as to illuminate the targets – accordingly factories and public buildings like schools had spotters posted on the roof who would raise the alarm and stop fires from spreading. A lonely job and a nervy one …

> Fire-watching is a dreich job at the best of times, but in an engine shop it's inclined to be just a little frightening. Familiar things take on new shapes. Wall cranes become gibbets, and if there is a sling suspended from the hook it sways in the breeze that is never absent and queasily reminds you of boyhood tales wherein highwaymen were justly suspended at some forlorn spot on the turnpike.

In the immediate aftermath of the March bombing the Corporation of Glasgow advertised the availability of ('free of charge') air-raid shelters to householders. These were of two main types: (1) Outdoor brick or steel shelters, capable of accommodating between four and ten persons, to be erected in gardens or other suitable ground attached to houses other than tenement houses; (2) Indoor shelters for ground-floor houses only, capable of accommodating two adults and one child or two adults and two small children.

Note that the effectiveness of the policy depended on individuals making requests. Many of the existing Anderson shelters had been acquired and erected by individual householders in a pretty random fashion. However, by 16 April the Corporation had received 1,000 applications for indoor shelters – these were normally called Morrison shelters, after the government minister Herbert Morrison. They were usually described as 'resembling tables' and had to be assembled by the householders themselves. The tenement dweller had recourse to the larger type of brick shelter, found in back greens. Bob Crampsey's splendid account of his growing up in wartime, *The Young Civilian*, includes this sketch of a family's experience in the Mount Florida area of Glasgow:

> Any security it provided was at best psychological since the shelters were hastily thrown-up brick constructions. Ours was always cold and dank and attempts to make it more cheerful only served to intensify the gloom. We hung mats across the door, not only to keep out the cold but to allow us to light torches and storm lamps. We

carried out chairs and sat in the weird light, jerkins and trousers pulled over pyjamas. We drank tea and ate sandwiches of the bread which was growing steadily darker as the war progressed. We were horribly fascinated by our first blitzed tenement with its great baulks of timber, glass everywhere and a bath perched precariously on the ruined third floor, lurching drunkenly against the still-bright pattern of the wallpaper.

So Glasgow and neighbouring towns were on the receiving end of a substantial bombing campaign, and this was not surprising, considering what a tempting target they presented. The docks, shipyards and engineering works together with the armaments factories themselves, grew in importance as the war progressed (see Chapter 11). Despite this, following the two-day Greenock blitz in the early May of 1941, the large-scale (200-bomber) German raids ceased. There are a number of reasons for this: the opening of the Eastern Front by the Russians. Secondly, the fact that the Clyde lay at the very edge of German bombers' range. At no point in the war did the Luftwaffe favour long range bombers – their preference for medium range versions was probably a reflection of the advantage gained by the occupation of mainland Europe and the ease with which bomber fleets could reach London, the prime target. Lastly, there were other softer targets which were available or seemed to be available to the Germans.

With reference to the first point, the full force of German bombing attacks on most British cities and ports was substantially lessened or perhaps even suspended at this point in the early summer of 1941. Hitler's sudden breaking of the non-aggression pact and launching of Operation *Barbarossa* against the Soviet Union deflected attention to a new Eastern Front just at the point when the raids were beginning to prove effective. Glasgow and the Clyde were spared the kind of fate that befell Hamburg and Dresden, or for that matter, London. The capital continued to endure continuous bombing and later bore the brunt of Hitler's V-Weapon attacks.

Contemporary reports make it clear that the need to rebuild housing and to a lesser extent industry after wartime damage from aerial bombardment was identified at an early stage in Glasgow, although reconstruction was to be a slow process extending well into the post-war period. The minister of works, Lord Reith, himself a Scot, visited in the immediate aftermath of the raids and conceded that the damage was worse than '... anything he had seen in any part of the country [but] was impressed with progress which was being made in the work of repair and reconstruction'.

Glasgow

GB 8320
Schiffswerft Henderson

A

B

D

C

Govan

GB 664
Azetylenwerk

G

E

F

Fig. 36 (opposite)

This is a close-up view of Fig. 35. Civilian casualties in Glasgow and Clydebank, as is well known, were very high in the March air-raids, while damage to industrial targets was comparatively light. *(Imperial War Museum)*

Fig. 37 (above)

Heinkel 111 bombers are seen flying in formation in this shot. The Heinkel was one of two types of bomber – the other being the Junkers 88 – that took part in the raids on Clydeside in March 1941. Even though the Heinkel had undergone heavy losses during the Battle of Britain in the latter half of 1940, and these long-range raids were unescorted by a fighter screen, German casualties were very light over the Clyde. Bomb-load and range were by this time inferior to the Junkers 88. The Heinkel had earlier played a pivotal role in Hitler's blitzkriegs on Poland, Norway and Denmark, and the working life of the aircraft was extended throughout the war. As late as the summer of 1944 they were in use as flying launch platforms for the V1 flying bombs. *(Imperial War Museum)*

GLASGOW: A CITY AT WAR

Fig. 38 (opposite)
Photographs of the blitz on Glasgow and Clydeside in March 1941 include this shot of rescue workers searching for survivors in the ruins of a tenement building in Kent Street, Glasgow. Apart from firemen, police and ARP workers, volunteers included miners from the Fife coalfields and off-duty servicemen.
(The Daily Record)

Fig. 39
An ARP worker rescues a little girl from a ruined building in the Clydeside Blitz of March 1941. Civilian casualties totalled more than 1,000, as, despite the high quality intelligence already noted, most bombs fell on housing areas.
(The Daily Record)

Fig. 40

Sailors on leave or waiting to join ships give assistance in clearing wreckage from a damaged building. The sailors' caps appear to be blanked out for security reasons.
(The Daily Record)

GLASGOW: A CITY AT WAR

Fig. 41 (opposite)
A famous view of a Glasgow Corporation tramcar that has sustained a direct hit from a German bomb or from flying debris from neighbouring buildings.
(The Daily Record)

Fig. 42 (top)
Two more tramcars of the Coronation type are shown in this view taken in the early morning following a raid. A rescue worker with a whistle on a lanyard stands by a makeshift road-block and directs the sparse traffic. Clouds of dust still hang everywhere.
(The Daily Record)

Fig. 43 (below)
Two children watch workmen clear away rubble.
(The Daily Record)

Fig. 44

Here domestic furniture from more lightly damaged homes stand in the street. By some freak the china cabinet and its contents appear unscathed.

(The Daily Record)

GLASGOW: A CITY AT WAR

Fig. 45 (top)
An air-raid warden holds two birdcages rescued from the bomb damage. The fate of the occupants is unclear.
(*The Daily Record*)

Fig. 46 (opposite)
The Govan Ferry is seen in use as a fire tender on the Clyde and fighting the fire on HMS *Sussex,* in September 1940. The firefighters are mainly in the upper level of the ferry. The view is taken from another vessel; note that the cruiser is listing considerably. As described elsewhere, fire crews, including those on the ferry, managed eventually to flood the magazine and avoid calamity.
(*Clydeport Archive*)

Fig. 47 (below)
Two workmen examine a bomb crater in Yarrow's shipyard. This was the result of rather more accurate targeting by the Luftwaffe. (Yarrow's wartime work is described in Chapter 11.)
(*BAE Systems*)

Fig. 48 (top)
Another view of the Govan ferry fire-fighting alongside HMS *Sussex*, taken from the dockside. *(Clydeport Archive)*

Fig. 49 (below)
HMS *Sussex* is shown here at her moorings, this time at Scapa Flow in Orkney, following earlier battle damage. *(Imperial War Museum)*

Fig. 50

A view of a large
unexploded, but
presumably unarmed
bomb at Rothesay Dock,
with dock officials, in the
weeks following the first
Clydeside Blitz.
(Clydeport Archive)

Fig. 51
A bomb squad is seen here with an unexploded bomb (UXB) at Rothesay Dock in April 1941.
(Clydeport Archive)

13.3.41
ROTHESAY
DOCK
3.4.41.

[6]

WARTIME VISITORS

In both world wars Glasgow saw many visitors, both the world famous and the very ordinary. Of course the city's role as a major centre of defence production made much of the official visiting very natural; although one distinguished naval officer, Vice Admiral Sir James Troup, Flag Officer Glasgow for most of the Second World War, rather cynically noted a remarkable tendency for official visitors to avoid Glasgow during the winter months and also felt that whenever Whitehall was at a loss to know what to do with a distinguished personage their answer was to pack them off to Glasgow and Clydeside for a few days!

Glasgow's visitors included huge numbers of British, Commonwealth and foreign troops, many of whom passed through the city briefly on their way to camps, airfields and depots elsewhere in the British Isles, or were being shipped out of Glasgow on their way to an overseas theatre of operations.

Some military visitors were in and around the Glasgow area for longer periods of time – this was especially true of the forces of our Allies who had found sanctuary here after the occupation of their own countries. For example the French troops evacuated from the ill-fated Norwegian campaign in spring 1940 or the large numbers of Polish soldiers, sailors and airmen who were based in and around Glasgow and with whom the city, and not least its Lord Provost, Patrick Dollan, established a very special relationship.

In June 1917 the Prime Minister, David Lloyd George, came to Glasgow to receive the freedom of the city. This decision had been unpopular with many of the left-wing organisations in Glasgow, who recalled his role as Minister of Munitions and the controversy over dilution (see Chapter 3). Willie Gallacher wrote in *Revolt on the Clyde* that the Council's decision to honour Lloyd George 'had aroused fury at all working-class meetings' and a vociferous protest was raised on the day of the ceremony: 'We had no general stoppage on the Clyde, but we succeeded in getting large numbers to cease work and to demonstrate from early morning.'

Royalty paid visits to Glasgow in both wars and indeed these visits were in some ways the forerunners of the more populist 'meet the people' type of royal

Fig. 52

One of the royal visits to Glasgow during the Second World War was a two-day visit in June 1942. On the second day of this visit King George VI and Queen Elizabeth sailed down the Clyde to inspect the war industries of the river. They boarded TSS *Queen Mary II* at Bridge Wharf in the centre of Glasgow for their trip. Our photograph shows the queen with the Flag Officer, Glasgow, Vice Admiral Troup.
(Imperial War Museum)

visit to which we have become accustomed in recent years. King George V's visit to Glasgow in 1917 included the unprecedented event of an outdoor investiture at Ibrox Stadium when three Victoria Crosses were presented together with honours in the newly created Order of the British Empire.

At the conclusion of his visit, during which he slept in the royal train, parked at Kirklee Station near the city's Botanic Gardens, the king wrote to Lord Provost Sir Thomas Dunlop, and recalling that this had been his third visit to the city in as many years, remarked:

> I am pleased to see that, if possible, there is more determination than ever in the spirit and fortitude of the people of this famous industrial centre to support the heavy task of my sailors and soldiers.
>
> The security of our food supply cannot be taken as a matter of course, and the main object of my tour was for the purpose of showing the great interest I take in the efforts of those employed in shipyards and steel mills to maintain the strength and efficiency of our mercantile marine, on which the very existence of this country depends.

Many of the more ordinary visitors to Glasgow found a warm welcome in the city and established relationships that endured for life. Perhaps the most famous examples of this came in the Second World War 'G.I. Brides' boom, when many local girls who had met and fallen in love with American servicemen sailed off to the United States to start a new life with their American husbands. Even where such romantic entanglements did not arise, the arrival of American troops in austerity Glasgow had a huge impact. Unheard-of luxuries such as nylon stockings, chocolate and chewing gum brightened up the war-time lives of many Glasgow families, living on meagre rations in a cold, blacked-out city. The inclusion of black GIs in the American forces brought a novel element into the city's social mix – and one which had its difficulties. The US forces were racially segregated, a policy which was unfamiliar, not to say unwelcome, to the host community. At events arranged by the host community there was often some degree of tension because the black GIs were integrated into dances and other entertainments.

As a great seaport Glasgow, and the Clyde, welcomed many travellers and sheltered many survivors from the perils of the sea – including the survivors of the *Athenia* – the first sinking of the Second World War. The arrival of the *Athenia* survivors resulted in the US Ambassador sending his twenty-two-year-old son to Glasgow to meet the survivors. The son was to become rather better known than the father and became the 35th President of the United States, John F. Kennedy.

Glasgow was also the location for one of the most significant moments in British American relations during the Second World War. John Kennedy's father, Joseph Kennedy, was deeply pessimistic about the prospects of Britain surviving Hitler's assault after the fall of France, let alone winning the war. His official reports to Washington argued against American aid. President Franklin Roosevelt despatched a trusted adviser, Harry Hopkins, to give him a first-hand account of Britain and a confidential assessment of its chances to set against the official line coming from the Ambassador. Hopkins met with Prime Minister Winston Churchill and toured various sites including the Home Fleet base at Scapa Flow. Hopkins had been silent throughout his travels and could not be drawn on his impressions of Britain's ability and willingness to resist or on the nature of the message he was going to take back to his President. Churchill and Hopkins arrived in Glasgow where Churchill had asked the Civil Defence Commissioner for Scotland, Tom Johnston, to arrange a private dinner. Johnston, who must rank as one of the greatest Scots of the twentieth century, was a Labour MP, who shortly afterwards was persuaded to become Secretary of State for Scotland in Churchill's coalition government.

The dinner was held in Glasgow's North British Hotel on 17 January 1941 and after speeches from Churchill and Johnston the latter, on impulse, called on Hopkins to speak. Hopkins' brief speech, in which he pointed out that he was here on a fact-finding mission for Roosevelt, ended with a paraphrase of famous words from the Old Testament Book of Ruth: 'Wheresoever thou goest we go, and where thou lodgest we lodge, thy people shall be our people, thy God, our God, even unto the end.' Johnston, in his memoirs, records that 'Churchill's eyes welled up in tears. Here was the first news that the United States was throwing its weight upon the Allied side.'

Some foreign visitors saw Glasgow on a number of occasions – King Haakon VII of Norway, forced to flee his country in the face of German invasion, landed at Greenock and was welcomed by Vice Admiral Troup in June 1940. Later he was able to return to the city, and to launch a ship for the Norwegian government at the Whiteinch shipyard of Barclay Curle.

Of course not all foreign visitors were quite so welcome – a steady stream of prisoners of war passed through the city on their way to interrogation centres, prisoner of war camps and hospitals. Perhaps the most celebrated of these visitors was the Deputy Führer Rudolf Hess, who made a (still-controversial) flight to Scotland, apparently to discuss peace terms with the Duke of Hamilton. Hess crash-landed on the outskirts of the city, was found injured by an Eaglesham ploughman, was taken into custody by the Home Guard and then removed to a Glasgow hospital and later transferred to Maryhill Barracks.

Fig. 53

At the end of his 1917 tour of Glasgow and Clydeside, a tour which had taken him round factories, steel mills, shipyards and munitions plants in the city and in Renfrewshire and Lanarkshire, King George V arrived on 20 September by train at Central Station and met officers and men of the merchant service, whose ships had been lost due to enemy action during the war. The king then went on to conclude his Clydeside tour with visits to the engine works of Dunsmuir and Jackson, the Fairfield shipyard and the Renfrew yards of Messrs W. Simon & Co and Messrs Lobnitz. *(Imperial War Museum)*

GLASGOW:
A CITY AT WAR

Fig. 54

This photograph shows
King George V on a visit to
the Meadowside shipyard
of D. & W. Henderson on
18 September 1917. This
firm, established in 1873,
had had a long association
with the Anchor Line.
During the First World War
the firm became the lead
yard for two models of
War Standard cargo ships
which could be turned out
quickly and cheaply to
meet the demands of the
war and replace the
growing number of cargo
vessels sunk by enemy
action. King George knew
the work of Henderson's
yard – his racing yacht
Britannia had been built
there in 1893 for his father,
the Prince of Wales, later
Edward VII – indeed the
king told a partner in the
firm that the *Britannia* was
still as strong as when it
had left his yard.
Henderson's was a
remarkably versatile yard,
turning out tramp steamers
and Atlantic liners such as
the *Columbia*, yachts and
large sailing ships.
(Imperial War Museum)

Fig. 55

The sinking of the Donaldson Line's *Athenia* off Ireland on 3 September 1939 with the loss of
112 lives was a clear breach of the German Navy's own rules of engagement and the Hague
Conventions. The survivors of the sinking were brought to Glasgow. Many of them were
Americans and the US Ambassador in London, Joseph P. Kennedy, sent his son Jack north to
represent him. The photograph taken on 7 September outside the sandbagged entrance to
Glasgow's Central Hotel shows the unmistakeable figure of the future President with a group of
survivors. Standing to the left of Kennedy as you look at the photograph is the Lord Provost of
Glasgow, Patrick Dollan. *(James Hall)*

Fig. 56

Large numbers of Polish troops found their way to Scotland after the fall of Poland and the relations between them and Glasgow were cordial. Much of the credit for this must go to Lord Provost Dollan, who took a great interest in the fate of Poland and in the welfare of the Polish servicemen in and around the city. On 31st August 1940 Dollan presented new colours to the 9th Lancers Regiment of the Polish Army as a gift from the City of Glasgow. Present at this ceremony, held at Biggar, were the Polish President Raczkiewicz and the Prime Minister and Commander in Chief of Polish Forces, General Sikorski.

The Polish Army Choir, under their conductor Lieut. J. Kolaczkowski, gave a series of concerts in and around Glasgow. One, in aid of the City of Glasgow's Central War Fund, featured the famous Irish lyric tenor John McCormack, accompanied by the equally distinguished pianist Gerald Moore. Our photograph shows the members of the choir outside Glasgow City Chambers.
(Kevin Morrison Collection Glasgow Caledonian University)

*Nazi Leader Flies
To Scotland*

Daily Record
and Mail.

BASSETTS ORIGINAL LIQUORICE ALLSORTS

ESTAB. 1847—No. 29,420   TUESDAY, MAY 13, 1941   E   ONE PENNY

RUDOLF HESS IN GLASGOW HOSPITAL

Herr Hess, Hitler's right - hand man, has run away from Germany and is in Glasgow suffering from a broken ankle. He brought photographs to establish his identity.

An official statement issued from 10 Downing Street at 11.20 last night said:—

"Rudolf Hess, Deputy Fuhrer of Germany and Party Leader of the Nationalist Socialist Party, has landed in Scotland under the following circumstances:

"On the night of Saturday, the 10th, a Messerschmitt 110 was reported by our patrols to have crossed the coast of Scotland and be flying in the direction of Glasgow. Since a Messerschmitt 110 would not have the fuel to return to Germany this report was at first disbelieved.

"Later on a ME.110 crashed near Glasgow with its guns unloaded. Shortly afterwards a German officer who had baled out was found with his parachute in the neighbourhood suffering from a broken ankle.

"He was taken to a hospital in Glasgow, where he at first gave his name as Horn, but later on he declared he was Rudolf Hess.

"He brought with him various photographs of himself at different ages, apparently in order to establish his identity. These photographs were deemed to be photographs of Hess by several people who knew him personally.

"Accordingly an officer of the Foreign Office who was closely acquainted with Hess before the war, has been sent up by aeroplane to see him in hospital."

A later official statement said Hess has been identified beyond all doubt.

THIS WAS HIS 'PLANE

Two pictures of the wreckage of the Messerschmitt 110 in which Rudolf Hess flew to Scotland.

"Insanity" —Rubbish

THE flight of Hess must have tremendous repercussions in Germany, where he was not only powerful but immensely popular, writes a Press Association political correspondent.

Although there is no official comment, the Berlin attempt to anticipate the news by speaking of Hess's "mental disorder" won't hold water, and there is every reason for drawing the conclusion that the flight was a deliberate one.

And Hess, significantly, chose a 'plane which would not have enough petrol to take him back.

It requires possession of all one's faculties to fly a fast fighting 'plane and "hallucinations" are not associated with piloting such a machine to a given point. The possession of photographs for identity purposes indicate that Hess knew where he was going.

Rudolf Hess

"I Found German Lying In Field"

DAVID M'LEAN, A PLOUGHMAN, WAS THE MAN WHO FOUND RUDOLF HESS. HERE IS M'LEAN'S OWN STORY AS TOLD TO THE "DAILY RECORD," FIRST NEWSPAPER ON THE SCENE:—

"I was in the house and everyone else was in bed late at night when I heard the 'plane roaring overhead. As I ran out to the back of the farm, I heard a crash, and saw the 'plane burst into flames in a field about 200 yards away.

"I was amazed and a bit frightened when I saw a parachute dropping slowly earthwards through the gathering darkness. Peering upwards, I could see a man swinging from the harness.

Good Morning! Another Day Nearer Victory!

Fig. 57 (above)

Hess's specially modified ME110 fighter crash-landed at Eaglesham, outside Glasgow. Hess was found by a local farmer, turned over to the Home Guard and after hospital treatment for his injuries was transferred to Maryhill Barracks. The timing of Hess's mission is of course significant. It took place just over a month before the start of Operation Barbarossa – the German invasion of the Soviet Union, a plan to which Hess must have been privy. Hess's flight, his motives, his mental stability, his fate (he was tried at Nuremberg as a War Criminal and imprisoned in Spandau Prison, Berlin until his suicide in August 1987 at the age of ninety-three) are all highly controversial and have attracted a huge literature. Evidence has been produced to suggest that the Spandau prisoner was not Hess and that the real Hess was killed and a substitute arranged to stand trial and be imprisoned in his place. Others argue that the Spandau prisoner, whether Hess or a substitute, was murdered rather than committed suicide. *(Daily Record)*

Fig. 58 (opposite)

The news of the flight of a leading member of the Nazi hierarchy to Britain was naturally a major news story just as soon as censorship allowed. Hess crashed on Saturday 10 May and the story was released to the press on the evening of Monday 12 May. It was a 'good news' story at a time when good news was in very short supply: Greece and Yugoslavia had just been overrun by the Germans and British forces were being besieged in Tobruk.

His claimed mission was to meet, in the first instance, the Duke of Hamilton, and through his assumed good offices, open up discussions with the British Government about peace. Hess had met the duke, then the Marquess of Clydesdale (he only inherited the ducal title on his father's death on 16 March 1940) at the Berlin Olympics in 1936 and felt that he would make an appropriate British contact. Hess planned to fly his ME110, which had been fitted with additional fuel tanks, from the Messerschmitt factory airfield near Augsburg, Bavaria to Dungavel, Ayrshire, a private landing strip near the Duke of Hamilton's house. However Hess who was, like the Duke of Hamilton, an experienced pilot, found the Dungavel strip unlit and with dwindling fuel was obliged to carry out his first parachute jump – and injured his leg on landing. *(Daily Record)*

GLASGOW: A CITY AT WAR

Fig. 59 (right)
An un-named Polish airman feeds the pigeons in Glasgow's George Square. If he had been in the city in September 1940 he might well have attended the international football match between a British Army XI and a Polish Army XI. This was held at Partick Thistle's Firhill Park, and resulted in a 4–0 victory for the home side.
(Kevin Morrison Collection Glasgow Caledonian University)

Fig. 60 (opposite)
The Norwegian government in exile had to reconstitute its navy and merchant marine, most of which had been seized or sunk in the German invasion of Norway in the spring of 1940. A tramp ship *Empire Penn* which was building at Barclay Curle's Whiteinch yard for the British Ministry of War Transport was transferred to the Norwegian government and re-named *König Haakon VII*. She was in fact the first merchant ship to be handed over to an Allied government from a British shipyard in replacement of tonnage lost in the Allied cause. Sadly the launch, by Mrs Sunde, the wife of the Norwegian Minister of Supply (seen with King Haakon VII in the picture), was marred by a post-launch accident. The *König Haakon VII* slid down the ways and ran into the Blue Funnel Line's *Myrmidon* on her way up-river to discharge cargo at Princes' Dock. Both ships sustained considerable damage. *König Haakon VII* sailed in Atlantic and Russian convoys and at the end of the war was engaged in transporting prisoners of war of various nationalities home to their countries of origin – German troops from north Norway to Bremerhaven, Russians to Murmansk, French soldiers captured on the Eastern Front from Tromsø to Cherbourg. Later she passed into Panamanian and Phillipine ownership and was broken up at Kaohsiung, Taiwan, in July 1972. *(James Hall)*

[7]

THE RAF AND AIR DEFENCES

The story of the involvement of Glasgow in aerial warfare is of course dominated by the city's experiences during the blitz of 1941. Chapter 4 deals with Glasgow on the receiving end of German bombing raids in March and May of that year. Before that, however, Glasgow had already made a crucial contribution to the effectiveness of the Royal Air Force, and this chapter is primarily the story of 602 Squadron, the City of Glasgow Air Squadron.

The squadron had been the first of twenty-one auxiliary squadrons to be formed (in 1925) within the Royal Air Force and began flying from Moorpark Aerodrome at Renfrew. It was originally a bomber squadron but converted to fighters in May 1939. One of its peacetime pilots had been the Marquess of Douglas and Clydesdale (later the Duke of Hamilton), who had a connection with the Rudolf Hess affair, as described in Chapter 6.

Such was the confidence of the Air Ministry in this unit that 602 was the first Auxiliary Squadron to be equipped with Spitfires – and, indeed, seventh in the whole Royal Air Force. Spitfires were flown into the Abbotsinch aerodrome to be fitted with their guns and subjected to modifications to their Merlin engines at the conveniently located Rolls Royce Aero Engine Plant at Hillington. On the outbreak of war in September 1939, 602 had exhibited such a high degree of operational skill that the squadron was able to play a full part as a front-line operational unit. The City of Edinburgh Squadron and 602 were the first auxiliary units to go into action in October 1939 and 602 with its Spitfires was involved in the shooting down of the first German aircraft in UK skies.

In the late summer of the following year aerial warfare really began to gather momentum. Reichsmarschall Hermann Goering defined the objectives to his commanders of the German Air Fleet in August of 1940:

> The Führer has ordered me to crush Britain with my Luftwaffe. By delivering a series of very heavy blows I plan to have this enemy, whose morale is already at its lowest, down on his knees so that our troops can land without any risk.

Fig. 61

A Spitfire of 602 (City of Glasgow) Squadron is seen at Kenley aerodrome in 1941. The single-seat Supermarine Spitfire was of course *the* glamour fighter of the Second World War (indeed of any time) and was closely associated with 602, since they were the first auxiliary squadron to be equipped with them, shortly before the outbreak of war. The Spitfire had a ceiling of 34,000 feet and a speed of 312 mph, although late versions – it was the only British aircraft to remain in production throughout the war – could attain 450mph. There were more than forty versions in all and they were armed with various combinations of weapons – in this case with 20mm cannon. In this view the ubiquitous (virtually every British aircraft at the time was (continued overleaf)

GLASGOW: A CITY AT WAR

powered by it) British Rolls Royce twelve-cylinder Merlin engine is exposed for servicing. During the Battle of Britain the less glamorous Hawker Hurricane actually shot down considerably more enemy aircraft than did the Spitfire. The latter fighter had superior speed and manoeuvrability and generally went after German fighter escorts like the Messerschmitt 109, while the Hurricane acted as a 'gun platform' more effectively, seeking to intercept the waves of bombers heading for the capital and other vital targets. *(602 Squadron Museum)*

In other words, Britain was faced with invasion. And standing against invasion was the RAF. It was at this point that 602 Squadron moved south into the thick of the action of the Battle of Britain and soon established itself as one of the most renowned fighter squadrons. It achieved the second highest total of 'kills', the lowest pilot loss rate and was the longest serving squadron in the front line. At this point too Glasgow's pilots made a distinctive contribution to that aspect of the war that Angus Calder calls 'myth-making'. The squadron's pilots were among the 'Few'. This was Churchill's memorable term for the Spitfire and Hurricane fighter pilots, who, though greatly outnumbered by the attacking German bomber forces, achieved in the space of a few weeks a mythical status akin to medieval knights or champions – as far as the young Scottish pilots were concerned, a comparison might be made with Robert the Bruce on his palfrey contesting with De Bohun, before the opposed armies at Bannockburn.

The Battle of Britain, fought in the summer months of 1940, was 'won' by 602 and other fighter squadrons – at least in the sense that when it was over Hitler had to abandon plans for an invasion of Britain. However, it was by no means the end of German aerial attacks, and a significant change in the Luftwaffe tactics from daytime to night-time raids was in operation by the time of the Clydeside Blitz in the spring and early summer of 1941. There was a certain irony in that the March attacks were not opposed by a substantial defensive fighter force, even though 602 Squadron had temporarily returned to Prestwick from its successful stint in the south-east of England. The fact was, however, that the specialist night-fighters like the Defiants, Blenheims and Beaufighters were still in the process of being developed and the Spitfires were only partially equipped for interception of attackers during the hours of darkness. It was also true that night-fighter tactics had not been sufficiently worked out, as explained in *Lions Rampant*, a first-rate account of 602's history written by Douglas McRoberts.

Co-ordination of defence against the bombers was supposed to come about through agreement about the respective operational roles of the anti-aircraft batteries and the night-fighters. The fire from the A/A guns, according to Air Ministry instructions, operated up to or at a ceiling of 12,000 feet, while the British night-fighters were ordered up to a height above that. Between them there was a designated buffer zone, intended to ensure that the British planes were not hit by what would later be called friendly fire. In what developed into a very confused situation, though, the precise nature of the buffer zone was uncertain and the orders unclear – some reports held that the operating level for fighters such as 602 Squadron's Spitfires was set at 19,000 feet, others put the figure much lower. At any rate, very few interceptions were made and the

200-odd bombers came in over Glasgow and the Clyde at around 13,000 feet, almost untouched by anti-aircraft fire and unmolested by night-fighters.

> We fused the shells for 12,000. I could see ours bursting below the bombers. As far as I know we never hit a single one. I found my mother's tenement flattened. She was OK but I just remember feeling angry and helpless.
>
> *A/A Gunner, Glasgow*

The only enemy aircraft confirmed shot down during the Clydeside raids was on the Thursday night, when a Heinkel 111 was downed by a Blenheim flying from Turnhouse and equipped with a new radar interception device. Contact was made about six miles south of Glasgow when the Heinkel, carrying a bomb-load of incendiaries, was flying at 12,000 feet – after being hit it crashed near Dunure in Ayrshire.

Thus far, 602 and other fighter squadrons had filled an essentially defensive role as part of the 'Few'. The RAF now was able to move gradually from a defensive to an offensive role. The offensive directed at the cities and industries of Germany was mounted by the bomber squadrons that flew from English bases. The city of Glasgow was not directly involved in terms of men and materials, even if some of the strategic management of the vast airlift of bombers from Canada, and later and overwhelmingly from the USA, was carried out there. The destination for the armadas of US Flying Fortresses and Lancasters built under licence in Canada and sent onwards to the bomber bases, was of course the giant airfield at nearby Prestwick.

The offensive capabilities of the RAF also involved fighters such as Spitfires operating as strike aircraft aimed at specific European targets and in support of subsequent raids into Fortress Europe. The City of Glasgow Squadron had an important role to play in this also. After a spell at Prestwick and Ayr in early 1941, 602 returned south, flying strike sorties into Europe from Kenley and Redhill, and later provided fighter cover during the catastrophic Dieppe Raid in August 1942. In September the squadron again moved north to the Orkney and Shetland Islands (with one flight in each of the two groups of islands). Their mission was to intercept the high-level German reconnaissance raiders over Scapa Flow. They then flew from bases in the south of England from January 1943 and transferred to the Second Tactical Air Force in November, flying offensive sweeps over France and providing fighter escorts. Around this time, the squadron lost in action one of the few pilots who, at this point in the war, actually hailed from the city of Glasgow. He was Flight Sergeant George Hannah. Hannah was also a member of another interesting group – one of those non-commissioned pilots who had risen through the ranks to flight duties. In this instance, Hannah had joined up as an aircraft fitter and then volunteered for pilot training on the outbreak of war.

The squadron was involved in a crucial support role in the Normandy landings of June 1944. McRoberts' book gives a graphic description of the first day and the fighters' panoramic view of the Channel and the beaches on the American sector:

> *June 6th. D-Day. 08.15 hours.*
> The Channel shimmered in the morning night as the twelve Spitfires with the Lions Rampant swept in at 3,000 feet over the endless stream of shipping which stretched, like an enormous bridge, right back to the Isle of Wight. Soldiers and sailors waved at their protectors; the Glasgow pilots, keyed up, eased out into battle formation as they approached the coast between Cap de la Heve and the Cherbourg Peninsula. Not a sign of the Luftwaffe, but wherever they looked below, the battle raged.

Following the 'D' Day Invasion, 602 later flew from airfields in Normandy and other parts of Western Europe before returning to England in September 1944 to concentrate on strikes against the German V2 rocket sites and other prime targets. The huge supersonic V2s were of course launched into the stratosphere (an altitude of over 50,000 feet), and there could be no possibility of interception on the missiles' trajectory. The only hope was to attack the launch pads. Accordingly 602 Squadron's Mark XVI Spitfires were now adapted to a dive-bombing role. They slung 1,000 lb bombs under the fuselage, 250-pounders under the wings and attacked the concreted launch sites in and around The Hague in Holland. A successful low-level attack on a V2 complex in The Hague in March 1945 was among 602's last engagements before peace came on 8 May. The squadron disbanded soon after, on 15 May 1945, by which time it was credited with the destruction of 150 enemy aircraft during the hostilities.

The 602 Squadron Museum was officially opened on 22 October 1983 by Marshal of the Royal Air Force, The Lord Cameron of Balhousie. It was built to commemorate the outstanding achievements of No 602 (City of Glasgow) Squadron, Royal Auxiliary Air Force from its formation in 1925 until its disbandment in 1957. In addition to a wonderful collection of photographs, documentary evidence and memorabilia, the roll of honour, proudly displayed in the museum, records a momentous time in Britain's history.

Fig. 62

The great British airship R34 on Clydeside at the end of the First World War. The Germans had shown the usefulness of the airship and their Zeppelins had raided London and the east coast, including Edinburgh. Britain, too, developed the airship to a lesser extent and the R34, built by Beardmore's at the end of the war, might have had a significant military role, but her first flight did not take place until 20 December 1918. R34 was driven by five 250-horse power motors and measured 643 feet in length, while the total volume of her gas-filled bag was 1,950,000 cubic feet. Speed was not the main quality of the airship – the R34 flew at a stately 54 mph – but long range and endurance certainly was. In July 1919 the R34 left the East Fortune airfield in East Lothian and flew in just over 108 hours to New York. A few days later she re-crossed the Atlantic, this time in seventy-five hours with the aid of westerly winds and landed in Norfolk. Sadly the R34 was destroyed in an accident in 1921. The huge airship sheds seen in the background were demolished in the 1930s when a rubber factory was built on the Inchinnan site. *(Glasgow University Archive)*

Fig. 63

This is an evocative shot of a formation of 602 Squadron's Hawker Harts with Loch Lomond in the background. The fast and manoeuvrable Hart biplane, and its close relative the Hind, became the RAF's next standard light bombers after the Westlands, up until the late 1930s and the emergence of monoplanes such as the Fairey Battle and Bristol Blenheim. *(602 Squadron Museum)*

Fig. 64

A flight of the 602 (City of Glasgow) Air Squadron's Westland Wapitis are seen flying in formation in 1933. These medium bombers were the RAF's replacement between the wars for the De Havilland 9A (a veteran of the Great War) and were powered by the 500 hp Bristol Jupiter engine. In the version shown the fuselage and wings of the biplane are partially fabric-covered. 602 Squadron was an Auxiliary squadron and as such was subsequently equipped with the appropriately named Westland Wallace.

(602 Squadron Museum)

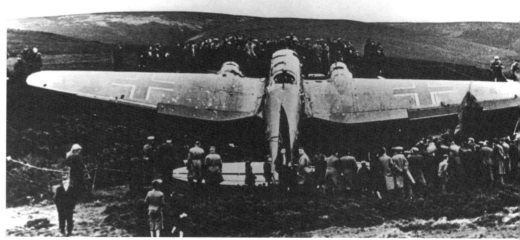

Fig. 65

This German Heinkel 111 bomber crash-landed in 1939 at Humbie, East Lothian, the first German raider to be shot down over land in World War Two. As described in Chapter 5, the Heinkel in bomber version was one of the German workhorses, although under-powered and under-armed in competition with most British fighters at this point in the air war. The Heinkel was engaged by Spitfires from 'Glasgow's Own' 602 Squadron in February 1940 – one of the pilots' reports reads: 'Enemy aircraft entered cloud and I followed'. As the photograph shows, the wreckage of the raider attracted large crowds of pressmen and curious spectators as well as police and other officials. *(602 Squadron Museum)*

Fig. 66

This photograph is a classic view of fighter pilots of the City of Glasgow 602 Squadron awaiting the order to scramble and engage the enemy during the Battle of Britain some time in the second half of 1940. At this stage in the hostilities the Glasgow squadron had been moved south close to the English Channel – the photograph was taken at a new airstrip at Westhampnett. The (mainly young) pilots are wearing their Mae West inflatable jackets – one pilot is wearing the insignia of a sergeant pilot, although the majority of what Churchill memorably called the 'Few' were officers. The pilot seated at the left is Findlay Boyd DSO DFC, who had at least twelve victories in combat, and behind him stands the young figure of Donald Jack – unusually, both survived the war. Note the fairly restrained pin-ups on the board behind.

(602 Squadron Museum)

Fig. 67

Squadron Leader, later Air Vice Marshal A.V.R. Johnstone DFC, is shown in this photograph. Johnstone was Commanding Officer of Glasgow's 602 Squadron in 1940/41, during the Battle of Britain. A Glaswegian himself, he was one of those who had served as pre-war auxiliary pilots and remained in service throughout the period from the outbreak of war until April 1941. As CO during the Battle of Britain he took the squadron south to engage the German aerial attackers of London, at a time when 602 accumulated a battle record that included the longest service in the front line, the second highest total of 'kills' and the award of more than a dozen Distinguished Flying Crosses. *(602 Squadron Museum)*

Fig. 68
The pilots of 602
Squadron and a Spitfire
are pictured in Normandy
in July 1944, after the
Allies had established a
foothold in France.
(Imperial War Museum)

GLASGOW:
A CITY AT WAR

Fig. 69

A Spitfire is pictured with its cockpit door open at Kenley in the following year, 1942. This example carries 602's famous Lion Rampant insignia, and also what is possibly the French cockerel emblem of Pierre H. Closterman DFC, one of several Free French pilots associated with 602. The crowbar on the inside of the door could be (and was) used to force open the cockpit cover in an emergency.

(602 Squadron Museum)

Fig. 70

In this photograph some of 602's ground crew are also seen in Normandy. This group was entirely made up of veterans from the Glasgow area. They are: (standing) Sergeant A.J. MacDonald of Govanhill Street, who has been with the squadron for fifteen years; Corporal W. Sweet of King's Park; LAC J. Gibson of Govan; LAC W. Douglas of Pollok Street; LAC A.F. Davis of Coatbridge; LAC C. Montgomery of Knightswood.

(Imperial War Museum)

Fig. 71

The pilots of 602 Squadron are pictured in Belgium planning an attack in the later part of the Second World War (probably in November 1944). As can be seen from the charts on display, the target was The Hague in Holland. This photograph was almost certainly released a considerable time after the action, for security reasons. The group includes (second left) Raymond Baxter, the post-war BBC broadcaster, and Glaswegian Tommy Love (third from right). The particular targets were V2 launch sites ringing the Hague. The V2 rocket was Hitler's most threatening 'secret weapon', which climbed to an altitude of 50,000 feet, before angling down towards London and the airfields of eastern England. Dive-bombing the V2 installations, it had been decided, was the only realistic course of action – interception at these supersonic speeds was deemed impossible. The allied squadrons involved were now equipped with the Spitfire XVI, armed with large bombs and operating like Stukas rather than fighters. A 602 ops record for 1 December, 1944 reads: 'Approaching The Hague, the bomb switches went to "on"; as they crossed the coast, the flak started, finding the range almost instantly. Max called, "Attacking – go! Go!", stood the Spitfire on her wingtip, and went vertically down. White bursts of flak streaked past … The next thing they saw was his bomb – exploding square on the V2 site in the corner of the Hague-Bosche park, right beside the former Royal Palace.'
(*602 Squadron Museum*)

[8]

TOTAL WAR

'Total War' is a largely twentieth-century phenomenon that has accompanied the growth of modern industrial societies. In this new kind of war, the civilian part of society is subject to many of the same hazards and dangers as the military. As has been suggested in Chapter 1, Glasgow has rarely been a battlefield and has generally been lucky to escape direct, immediate involvement in battlefronts (unlike Kilsyth, say, or Stirling). This remained true of nineteenth-century wars and of the First World War, although as we are reminded in Chapter 3, the city paid an enormous toll in the trenches of Flanders and on other war fronts, casualties that brought war home to almost every family. In addition, there was colossal hardship for Glasgow's civilian population, due to food shortages, for example. The Second World War saw better management of supply, although, as in the first great conflict of the century, there was a period when the U-boat menace came close to causing a complete strangulation of Britain's supplies. (The contribution of Glasgow and the Clyde to the defeat of that menace by the development of, amongst other things, the convoy system, was considerable.)

Many of the features of 'total war' are seen most clearly in the Second World War and they present themselves as certain indelible images, images seen very clearly in the context of the city of Glasgow and Clydeside. These images are very powerful and have endured in the public memory and consciousness. The images of 'the people's war' are associated with 'the home front: blitzed cities, communal air-raid shelters, the munitions factories of Britain's industrial heartlands and crowds of evacuees waiting for trains to take them to the relative safety of the countryside'.

All of the above were certainly visited upon Glasgow, even if it has been estimated that half of the Glasgow evacuees in 1939 had drifted back to the city by 22 November. And, of course, the blitz came later to Glasgow than to the cities of the south. As already indicated in Chapter 5, observers noted that the people of Glasgow felt 'a sense of relief at having been able to stand up to the ordeal [and] a new feeling of partnership with the English blitzed cities.'

Fig. 72

This evocative photograph, from 1941, shows a group of Rolls Royce women workers from the huge factory at Hillington (see Chapter 11). Second from left in the front row is Agnes McLean, a leader of the famous strike of women workers in that year protesting about the great anomaly between the wages of men and women workers. Out of a huge workforce of 22,000 people more than half were women, and yet they were (even the very skilled women) on a basic pay rate of 43s. a week, compared to the ordinary (unskilled) rate for men of around 73s. Even though strikes were technically illegal in wartime, the women staged a walk-out – as Agnes McLean recalled years later: 'It was a spontaneous strike, it wasn't, as far as we were concerned anyway, *(continued overleaf)*

GLASGOW: A CITY AT WAR

an organised well thought out strike ... we just one day got on our coats and walked out'. By 1943, following further industrial action, there was an improved grading system. However, real equality was many years off. *(The Gallacher Memorial Library, Glasgow Caledonian University)*

Another gauge of the 'totality' of war was the carrying through of National Registration of the entire civilian population on Friday 29 September 1939, just a few weeks after war broke out. The National Registration Identity Card was issued to all and was used for ID purposes and for the gradual imposition of rationing, particularly of food and of clothing.

Total war also means a state dedicating all or most forms of production to war purposes. Industrial production had to be continually raised in order to meet ever-expanding demand for munitions: tanks, guns, shells, and so on. In both world wars to a growing extent the greater part of society, including the agricultural and industrial sectors, was mobilised in support of the war effort. This happened more and more, the longer the war continued. For this to work, however, it was necessary that the workforce should be supportive.

Any consideration of wartime morale and appetite for 'dishing it out' to the enemy has to take account of certain well-known, if not notorious, characteristics of Clydeside workers, and chief among these was a reputation for militancy. Would this raise some doubt about the accuracy of a vision of a people united in the face of the enemy and of hardship?

In considering how this aspect of 'total war' might have looked in the context of the First World War, the Engineers' and Fairfields' wartime strikes of 1915 attracted much attention at the time and led to accusations of disloyalty or even treason. Much of the unrest was brought about by groups of skilled workers' deep distrust of Lloyd George's Munitions Act. It was perceived, particularly in Glasgow, as a threat that would lead to 'dilution' of labour as a result of the introduction of unskilled or semiskilled labour into the armaments industry. Lloyd George (shortly to become one of the great wartime prime ministers) was Minister of Munitions in 1915. He got a rough reception when he visited Glasgow to address the Clyde engineering workers, not least from the Socialist weekly, *Forward*, edited by a young Kirkintilloch man, Tom Johnston. Here is an extract from the *Forward* report of the meeting in St Andrew's Hall on Christmas Day 1917 (Christmas Day was then, and for many years after, a normal working day for most industrial workers in Scotland):

> The best-paid munitions worker in Britain, Mr Lloyd George (almost £100 per week), visited the Clyde last week in search of adventure. He got it ...
> On rising to speak Mr Lloyd George was received with loud and continued booing and hissing. There was some cheering, certainly, and about a score of hats were waved in the area, but the meeting

was violently hostile. Two verses of 'The Red Flag' were sung before the Minister could utter a word. Owing to the incessant interruption and the numerous altercations going on throughout the hall, it was quite impossible to catch every word of Mr George's speech.

'My first duty,' he said, 'is to express regret to you because I could not address the meeting on Thursday.' At this stage a delegate stood upon a seat and endeavoured to speak. He only got the length of saying, 'Mr Lloyd George' when apparently he was pulled down. There were loud cries of 'free speech', and someone shouted: 'This is a meeting of trade union officials, not police officials', evidently hinting at the surprisingly large force of police in the hall.

Mr L-G continued '... to go on chaffering about a regulation here and the suspension of a custom there is just haggling with an earthquake. Workmen; may I make one appeal to you? [Interruption.] Lift up your eyes above the mist of suspicion and distrust. Rise to the height of the great opportunity now before you. If you do, you will emerge after this war is over into a future which has been the dream of many a great leader.' [Cheers, loud hissing and booing.]

Even though on this occasion Lloyd George was shouted down and the meeting broke up in disorder, the skilled engineering workers gradually came to accept that their industry was, after all, going to be 'diluted'.

Of course, none of these arguments, protests and demonstrations alludes to the matter of women working in the wartime industries, and none acknowledges that women were the instruments of the much feared 'dilution'. There was large-scale mobilisation of women into the forces and into the industrial complexes, and much evidence of this was found on Clydeside. A *Glasgow Herald* report of the Armistice in 1918 contains references to 'munitions girls' that suggests widespread acceptance of their existence. Women became involved in war work in many fields of employment and this book contains several illustrations of Glasgow women in both world wars, employed not only in the armaments industry but also the service industries. They took such jobs as tram guards and even drivers, in an initiative devised by the famous General Manager of Glasgow Corporation Tramways, Mr James Dalrymple.

In the Second World War, recruitment of women was even more systematic. By 1943 compulsory recruitment of women into civil defence, munitions or the women's services had raised the number of women in the workforce by one and a half million. Not all women, of course, were engaged in war work – many of the middle classes, for example, found a

sense of involvement in the voluntary sector – not least in providing the famous morale-boosting cups of tea. The blitz of March 1941 was a watershed in bringing home the scope and horrors of global war directly to the people of Glasgow. A 'women's topics' feature in the *Herald* a few days after the bombing reflects this, as well as the role played by women in building, not just boosting, morale:

> We know it all now. It had been hearsay before. We had heard of raids and devastation; we had heard first-hand reports and thought we knew all about it. And all the time, even the most sensitively imaginative among us, we knew nothing. But down Clydeside way that is all changed now.

To return to the question of whether a sense of national unity was always apparent on the home industrial front: in the weeks following the March '41 blitz, newspapers carried news of a full-blown industrial dispute that had flared up over the introduction of a new dock labour scheme. In the shipyards around the same time there was an apprentice strike – another manifestation of industrial relations that fed the persisting legend of Red Clydeside. On the whole, in the Second World War, Glasgow had noticeably less strife in the field of industrial relations than before – this was more of a 'people's war'. The strikes mentioned above were short-lived, and accordingly were less threatening to wartime production. Ernest Bevin as Minister of Labour (with impeccable trade union credentials) and Tom Johnston as Secretary of State for Scotland (the same Tom Johnston who had helped to make things so hot for Lloyd George in the earlier conflict) were much more successful in creating a climate of co-operation. Bevin indeed was the most influential minister on the Home Front, and he worked with rather than against the unions in improving conditions and regulating working practices. In any case, in the conditions of utmost secrecy that obtained it is difficult to say how much industrial unrest actually affected the day-to-day administration of workplaces such as the King George V Dock. Another factor worth mentioning is that workers' attitudes began to change when the Soviet Union came into the war on the same side as Britain and when the workers of the Clyde found themselves, as it were, fighting alongside their Soviet comrades.

Another quotation from the newspaper feature seems to confirm the suppositions or hopes implicit in the phrase 'The People's War'. It runs:

> [The term] Clydebuilt has hitherto applied to its ships. All that it implies in rugged strength and reliability in times of stress has been

won by its people this past week … Perhaps Clydeside will one day play a prominent part in achieving the hope of the world. At the moment, Clydebuilt stands for a dour determination that no enemy will ever wrest from it, its own sturdy independence.

The prediction made above was fulfilled when Glasgow and Clydeside became intimately involved in the great land and sea operations (like *Torch*) that from 1942 wrested the initiative from the enemy and carried the fight to his strongholds – it did indeed play a prominent part in fulfilling victory or 'the hope of the world'.

Fig. 73
In the twentieth century, as part of the emergence of the concept of 'total war', traditional roles of all people in society were challenged, but none more than those of women. Here is a First World War woman street lamplighter working for Glasgow Corporation. The pole is used to ignite the street lamps, which were of course still gas lamps at this period. In 1915, when this photograph was taken, she was one of eighty women doing this job. In this case women took over what was previously regarded as men's work, because the men had moved into the armed forces. This situation was different from the use of women to 'dilute' employment, as in the case of some munitions workers. The lamplighters earned between 17s. and 28s. a week and worked for 51 hours. The photograph is from an album called 'Women's War Work – Corporation of Glasgow'. (*Imperial War Museum*)

Fig. 74

Female tram guards (not yet dubbed 'clippies') from the first World War pose in front of a tramcar, also belonging to Glasgow Corporation. This innovation, thought to be shocking by many at first, was the work of the well-known Tramways General Manager, Mr J. Dalrymple. The recruiting poster for the Bantams on the tramcar refers to the special regiments of men of below average height – Glasgow being a fertile recruiting ground for these.
(Mitchell Library, Glasgow)

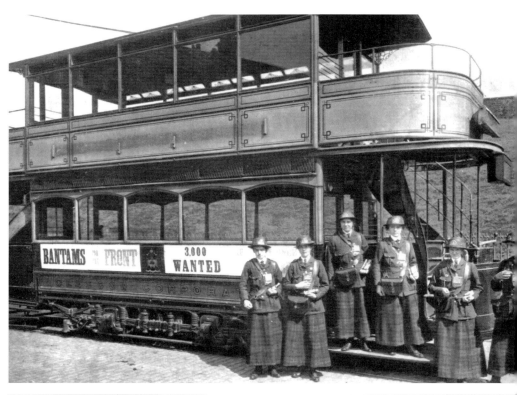

Fig. 75

A Mrs Turner (wearing the cap), a female tram driver, appears in this Second World War photograph. She is posing with an inspector and a male and female conductor, with whistles.
(Imperial War Museum)

Fig. 76
Some of the Yarrow Shipyard's female workers are seen at a metal pressing machine. Note the high standard of protective clothing and footwear.
(BAE Systems)

Fig. 77
Some more of Yarrow's women employees are engaged in flanging sheet metal for ventilation trunking. Yarrow was a major supplier of warships in the Second World War.
(BAE Systems)

Fig. 78
A fine study of soldiers and sailors at a mobile canteen in Glasgow in April 1940.
(The Daily Record)

Fig. 79

Members of the National
Fire Service are seen on
parade at their Glasgow
headquarters. The service
had an important role
during the Clydeside Blitz
in co-ordinating the
efforts of rescue workers.
*(Kevin Morrison
Collection, Glasgow
Caledonian University)*

Fig. 80

Lord Provost Patrick Dollan at the opening of a YMCA canteen in Glasgow's Central Station,
with staff and customers, drawn from the services and voluntary agencies. Like Secretary of State
for Scotland Tom Johnston, Dollan was a former neo-revolutionary Labour man who became
what we would now call an establishment figure. He had, for example, criticised his own
Glasgow Burgh Labour Party, for issuing a call (in November 1939) for peace rather than war.
He accused them of 'reacting to influence from Moscow' and being at odds with the policy of
the national party and of the TUC. Dollan had been a pacifist in the First World War, but
maintained that 'circumstances this time were entirely different'. *(The Daily Record)*

Fig. 81

A so-called Bevin Panel meeting in August 1940. Like similar meetings around the country, these panels met at Employment or Labour Exchanges to identify shortages of skilled employees and fill the vacancies from the pool of unemployed. By 1941 industrial control by government extended to the point where the Minister of Labour, Ernest Bevin, had extensive powers over labour mobility, worker discipline, conditions, hours and wages. Bevin (1881–1951) had had a distinguished career as General Secretary of the influential Transport and General Workers Union from 1921 to 1940. He became Minister of Labour in 1940 and made an immense contribution to the post-war restructuring of the social services, the creation of the Welfare State and the economy. *(The Daily Record)*

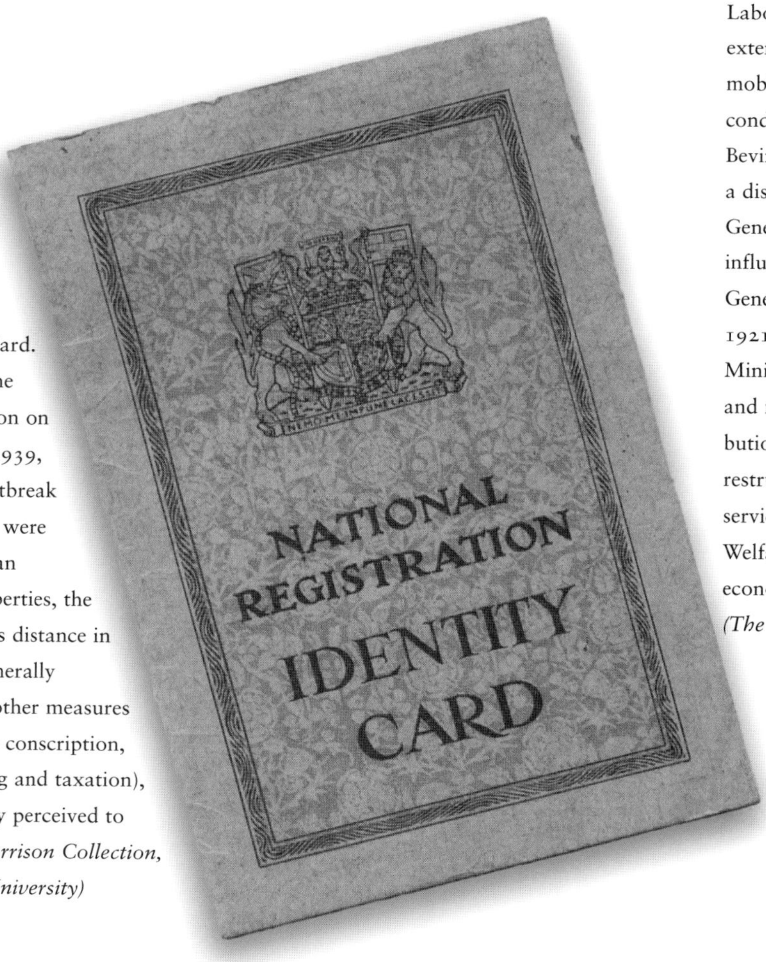

Fig. 82

A wartime National Registration Identity Card. These were issued to the entire civilian population on Friday, September 29 1939, within weeks of the outbreak of war. Although there were some who saw this as an infringement of civil liberties, the people seem – from this distance in time – to have been generally accepting of this (and other measures of state control such as conscription, rationing, requisitioning and taxation), because it was generally perceived to apply to all. *(Kevin Morrison Collection, Glasgow Caledonian University)*

[9] THE ARMY

Inscribed on the Cenotaph in Glasgow's George Square are two remarkable and significant statistics – one says that 8,654,465 persons served in the armed forces of the Crown in the First World War; the other notes that the City of Glasgow provided over 200,000 of this number. The epic scale of Glasgow's response to the call to arms was also given literary form in John Buchan's 1919 thriller *Mr Standfast*. The hero Richard Hannay comes to war-time Glasgow and reflects:

> As I made my way down the Dumbarton Road I was amazed at the number of able-bodied fellows about, considering that you couldn't stir a mile on any British front without bumping up against a Glasgow battalion. Then I realized that there were such things as munitions and ships, and I wondered no more.

Glasgow's local regiment was the Highland Light Infantry (HLI), formed in 1881 from an amalgamation of the 71st Highlanders and the 74th Highlanders, but the city also raised battalions for the Scottish Rifles as well as cavalry and artillery units and supporting arms, and of course Glaswegians served in every regiment and arm of the British Army.

There was usually at least a regular infantry battalion based at Maryhill Barracks (see the illustration in Chapter 1 of the presentation of new colours to the Gordon Highlanders). Maryhill Barracks was completed in 1872 to replace the old infantry barracks (built in 1795) in the Gallowgate. The 30-acre Maryhill Barracks complex was designed to house an infantry battalion and four artillery batteries. After Maryhill opened the Eglinton Street Cavalry Barracks (built in 1821) were closed.

Following the Cardwell reforms of 1881 most regular infantry regiments had two battalions, one of which was based in the UK, not necessarily in their home recruiting area, and one in an overseas posting. In the years before 1914 the 1st Battalion of the HLI (the former 71st) was based in India from 1905, while the 2nd HLI (the former 74th) was stationed in the UK.

Fig. 83

A group of combat-ready Highland Light Infantrymen riding into action on a Churchill tank somewhere in north-west Europe in the winter of 1944/45. The Churchill tank in its many variants and models was the main British armoured vehicle for much of the Second World War.
(Imperial War Museum)

ARM OF SERVICE	UNIT	HQ
Artillery	3rd Lowland Brigade, Royal Field Artillery	8 Newton Terrace
	4th Lowland (Howitzer) Brigade RFA	8 Newton Terrace
Cavalry	Lanarkshire (Queen's Own Royal Glasgow and Lower Ward of Lanarkshire) Yeomanry	Yorkhill Parade
Engineers	Glasgow Group Royal Engineers	21 Jardine Street
Infantry	Scottish Rifle Brigade	84 Robertson Street
	5th Battalion Scottish Rifles	261 West Princes Street
	7th Battalion (The Cameronians) Scottish Rifles	Victoria Road
	8th Battalion (The Cameronians) Scottish Rifles	149 Cathedral Street
	Highland Light Infantry Brigade	84 Robertson Street
	5th (City of Glasgow) Battalion HLI	24 Hill Street
	6th Battalion HLI	172 Yorkhill Street
	7th (Blythswood) Battalion HLI	69 Main Street, Bridgeton
	9th (Glasgow Highlanders) Battalion HLI	81 Greendyke Street
Medical	Royal Army Medical Corps (Territorial Force) Staff	Yorkhill Parade
	Lowland Mounted Brigade Field Ambulance	Yorkhill Parade
	1st Lowland Field Ambulance	Yorkhill Parade
	2nd Lowland Field Ambulance	Yorkhill Parade
	3rd Scottish General Hospital	Yorkhill Parade
	4th Scottish General Hospital	Yorkhill Parade
Services	Lowland Divisional Transport & Supply Column	22 Lochburn Road, Maryhill

In addition to regular battalions there were also the volunteer units of the Territorial Force. Glasgow had been a strong centre of the volunteer movement and when the Territorial Force was created in 1907, as a more effective and better-organised reserve for the Regular Army, this tradition continued. The local directory for 1914 lists the various battalions and units of the Territorial Force and gives an excellent overview of the Glasgow military tradition on the eve of what was to be its greatest test.

All these volunteer units drew their officers and men from the City of Glasgow (with the exception of one squadron of the Lanarkshire Yeomanry which, with a delightful lack of logic, was based in Paisley, Renfrewshire). As can be seen, Glasgow alone contributed the best part of a division to the Territorial Force. The city's units formed part of the Lowland Division, with particular strength in the supporting arms such as engineers and medical services, reflecting the industry of the city and the extensive medical expertise available in Glasgow's hospitals and university.

This extensive popular movement was mobilised in August 1914 on the outbreak of war in Europe:

His Majesty the King having been graciously pleased to order by proclamation that directions be given by the Army Council for embodying the Territorial Force, all men belonging to the said force are required to report themselves immediately at their headquarters.

As the *Glasgow Herald* wrote:

The man in the street has often been reproached for his apathy to the Territorials. Last night he turned round and looked with pride upon the men in uniform as they hurried through the streets to answer the King's call.

It went on to note:

The call to arms found the 5th Scottish Rifles ready. Their establishment is 28 officers and 976 other ranks, and about a month ago there were enrolled 27 officers and 801 other ranks. The news of mobilisation spread quickly, and throughout the afternoon and evening there were unwonted scenes of animation around the headquarters in West Princes Street. Large numbers of the battalion reported themselves and many former members came forward and signed the attestation paper for one or more year's service.

Most of the Glasgow Territorial Force units were just back from their annual summer training camps and were consequently in a high state of training and readiness. The movement of the Territorials to their summer camp was a highly complex operation involving special trains leaving Glasgow in the very early hours of the morning. In 1914 the HLI Brigade went to Gailes in

Ayrshire, along with the Glasgow Group of the Royal Engineers, the Transport and Supply Column and the RAMC. The Scottish Rifles Brigade went to Troon and the effect of these deployments was to turn a large part of the Ayrshire coast into a military camp.

The terms of engagement of the Territorial Force decreed that a Territorial soldier could only be sent out of the country with his consent – a consent which was to be freely given in the vast majority of cases. On 3 September General Patrick W. Henry, commanding the Highland Light Infantry Brigade, was able to write to the *Glasgow Herald* to advise its readers that his brigade (the 5th, 6th, 7th and 9th HLI) had been accepted for overseas service. He said that: 'Several men in each battalion, due to unfitness and other causes cannot in the meantime be accepted or get away, and it is desired ... to bring all the units up to war strength.' The general urged that Glasgow's recruiting efforts should be concentrated on filling up its own Territorial battalions. This emphasis on the local nature of recruitment – that men from the same town should fight together – was to prove extremely significant in the early stages of the First World War, although as the war wore on and the demand for manpower grew the principle was increasingly eroded.

Within a couple of weeks orders had been given to form reserve 'home service' units from those men who had not agreed to serve overseas. Many of Glasgow's Territorial units were swiftly sent overseas – for example the 9th HLI (The Glasgow Highlanders), which had been detached from the rest of the HLI Brigade, was in action on the Western Front by November 1914. Their comrades of the 5th, 6th and 7th Battalions landed in Gallipoli in July 1915.

The small British professional army which went to France in August 1914 (the 'contemptible little Army' of Kaiser Wilhelm's famous phrase), even reinforced by the fourteen divisions of the mobilised Territorial Force, was clearly not going to have the strength to cope with large scale European war. Lord Kitchener, the Secretary of State for War, realising the needs of a long war, which was not going to 'be over by Christmas', organised the creation of the 'New Army' and by September Glasgow's recruiting centres were thronged with men anxious to volunteer. The *Glasgow Herald* of 1 September reported that the recruiting offices in the Gallowgate and West Nile Street were particularly busy and that the police had to be called in to control the traffic. The Gallowgate office alone enlisted 256 men on Monday 30 August. The arrival of this flood of raw recruits produced a significant training problem and Kitchener issued an appeal to former non-commissioned officers to come forward and help train the battalions of the New Army.

The City Council agreed to raise and equip two battalions for Kitchener's New Army and the Glasgow Chamber of Commerce agreed to 'raise a battalion of commercial men for general service ... to be formed of men engaged as lawyers, accountants, stockbrokers, clerks, etc.'.

These units – of the type that came to be known as 'Pals Battalions' – became the 15th (Tramways), 16th (Boys Brigade) and 17th (Chamber of Commerce) Battalions of the Highland Light Infantry. The parenthetical descriptions never formed part of their official titles but reflected the predominant source of initial recruitment for these units. Whatever the advantages of the 'Pals Battalions' might have been in terms of morale, they had, in the high casualty environment of the Western Front, the effect of wiping out whole groups of men of the same background, or from the same district, or from the same occupation.

Four other HLI Battalions were raised for the New Army in 1914 and the 18th Battalion was raised by the City Council in February 1915 as a 'bantam' battalion. These battalions were created to use men who were below the standard height for enlistment, a type of man never hard to find in the streets of Glasgow, and the 18th HLI became part of the 35th (Bantam) Division and was serving in the Western Front by February 1916.

It would be impossible in a work of this nature to describe the movements of all the Glasgow units – and many Glaswegians served with distinction in non-Glasgow units. An example of the latter was Robert Downie, an employee of the North British Locomotive Works, who won the Victoria Cross for an action in France on 23 October 1916, while serving in the 2nd Battalion Royal Dublin Fusiliers. Sergeant Downie was one of 3,120 North British Locomotive men who joined the armed forces, 367 of them being killed in action. The service record of the city's own regiment – the Highland Light Infantry – can perhaps stand as a representation of Glasgow's military contribution to the Great War.

These battalions were filled over and over again as the attrition rate on the Western Front and in other combat areas increased. The 16th Battalion, to take one example, went into action on the Somme on 1 July 1916 with twenty-five officers and 755 other ranks – of whom only five officers and 221 other ranks were still alive and fit for service at the close of the day's fighting. Reinforced after these losses, two thirds of the 16th were lost at Beaumont-Hamel in November 1916.

The 9th HLI (The Glasgow Highlanders) fought throughout the campaign on the Western Front, perhaps most notably and tragically at High Wood on the Somme on 14/15 June 1916, where they formed part of the 33rd Division. A memorial in the form of a Highland cairn now stands

Highland Light Infantry Battalions on active service

FIRST WORLD WAR			
BATTALION NUMBER	CATEGORY	THEATRE OF WAR	PERIOD
1st	Regular Army	France (as part of 3rd Indian Division)	December 1914– November 1915
	Regular Army	Mesopotamia	1915–1918
2nd	Regular Army	Western Front (formed part of original British Expeditionary Force)	1914–1918
5th (City of Glasgow)	Territorial Force	Gallipoli and Middle East (as part of 52nd (Lowland) Division)	June 1915–April 1918
	Territorial Force	France	April 1918–Armistice
6th (City of Glasgow)	Territorial Force	As 5th	
7th (Blythswood)	Territorial Force	As 5th	
9th (Glasgow Highlanders)	Territorial Force	Western Front	November 1914– Armistice
10th	New Army	Western Front	1915–Armistice
11th	New Army	Western Front	1915–Armistice
12th	New Army	Western Front	1915–Armistice
14th (Bantam)	New Army	Western Front	1915–Armistice
15th (Tramways)	New Army	Western Front	1915–Armistice
16th (Boys Brigade)	New Army	Western Front	1915–Armistice
17th (Chamber of Commerce)	New Army	Western Front	1915–Armistice
18th (Bantam)	New Army	Western Front	1915–Armistice

In addition there were many other battalions, special reserve, home service, garrison, graduated and young soldiers battalions, some of which had a training role.

The 51st (Graduated) Battalion, formed from young recruits towards the end of the war was sent to Germany as part of the Army of Occupation.

at High Wood, formed from 192 stones, one for each man of the Glasgow Highlanders who died on that day.

One of the most popular of Glasgow fictional characters, J.J. Bell's 'Wee Macgreegor', enlists in the Glasgow Highlanders. In a remarkably realistic passage in one of the stories, 'Hullo, Glesca Hielanders', Bell conjures up a little of the horror and mixed emotions of war in the trenches:

Like a trodden, forgotten thing Private Macgregor Robinson lay on the Flanders mud, under the murk and rain. A very long time it seemed since that short, grim struggle amid the blackness and intermittent brightness. The night was still rent with noise and light, but the storm of battle had passed from the place where he had fallen. He could not tell whether his fellows had taken the enemy's trench or retired to their own. He had the vaguest idea as to where he was. But he knew there was pain in his left shoulder and right foot, that he was athirst, also that he had killed a man – a big, stout man, old enough to have been his father. He tried not to think of the last, though he did not regret it: it had been a splendid moment.

There were many deeds of heroism performed by the regiment in the Great War and seven Victoria Crosses were awarded to members of the HLI.

BATTALION	DATE	LOCATION	NAME OF RECIPIENT
2nd	1914	Verneuill	Private George Wilson
2nd	1914	Becelaere	Lieutenant Walter Lorrain Brodie
5th	1918	Moeuvres	Corporal David Ferguson Hunter
8th	1915	Givenchy	Lance Corporal William Angus (Attached Royal Scots)
9th	1917	Ypres	Lance Corporal John Brown Hamilton
12th	1918	Bois Favieres	Lieutenant Colonel William Herbert Anderson
17th	1916	Authuille	Sergeant James Youll Turnbull

Sixty-four battle honours were awarded to the HLI for services during the war. The regiment lost 598 officers and 9,428 rank and file were killed, died of wounds or died from disease in the course of the war.

The link between the HLI and Glasgow was strengthened in June 1923 when the regiment's name was changed to The Highland Light Infantry (The City of Glasgow Regiment). The regiment's depot had been moved from Hamilton to Maryhill Barracks in March 1921.

The inter-war years saw many changes in military matters and the situation in Glasgow reflected the new concerns, the more technical and mechanised nature of war, and the threat from the air.

The 1939 listing of Glasgow's Territorial Army units (the name had

ARM OF SERVICE	UNIT	H.Q.
Artillery	80th (Lowland) Field Regt. Royal Artillery	21 Taylor Street, Townhead
	74th Anti-Aircraft Regt. Royal Artillery	29 West George Street
	83rd Anti-Aircraft Regt. Royal Artillery	69 Main Street, Bridgeton
	14th Light Anti-Aircraft Regt. Royal Artillery	—
	54th (Queen's Own Royal Glasgow Yeomanry) Anti-Tank Regiment	51 Yorkhill Parade
	54th Searchlight Regt. Royal Artillery	261 West Princes Street
	57th Searchlight Regt. Royal Artillery	27 West George Street
Engineers	103rd (Glasgow) Army Troops Coy.	22 Lochburn Road, Maryhill
	109th (Glasgow) Workshop and Park Coy.	22 Lochburn Road, Maryhill
Infantry	7th Batt. The Cameronians (Scottish Rifles)	35 Coplaw Street, Victoria Park
	5th Batt. The Highland Light Infantry (The City of Glasgow Regiment)	24 Hill Street, Garnethill
	6th Batt. The Highland Light Infantry (The City of Glasgow Regiment)	172 Yorkhill Street
	9th (Glasgow Highlanders) Batt. Highland Light Infantry (The City of Glasgow Regiment)	Hotspur Street, Maryhill
Medical	156th (Lowland) Field Ambulance Royal Army Medical Corps	261 West Princes Street
	4th (Scottish) General Hospital RAMC	8 Newton Terrace
	5th (Scottish) Hygiene Coy. RAMC	41 Yorkhill Parade
Ordnance	52nd (Lowland) Divisional Ordnance Coy. Royal Army Ordnance Corps	8 Newton Terrace
Signals	52nd (Lowland) Divisional Signals	21 Jardine Street
	No. 3 Coy. 3rd Anti-Aircraft Divisional Signals	208 Renfrew Street
	GHQ Signals Supplementary Reserve	—

SECOND WORLD WAR

BATTALION	CATEGORY	THEATRE OF WAR	DATES
1st	Regular Army	France (with BEF)	1939–Dunkirk
	Regular Army	UK: Training	May 1940–June 1944
	Regular Army	North Western Europe	June 1944–VE Day
2nd	Regular Army	Palestine, Egypt & North Africa	1939–1942
	Regular Army	Sicily, Yugoslavia, Albania, Greece, Italy	1943–VE Day
5th	Territorial Army	France (52nd (Lowland) Division)	June 1940
		UK: Training	June 1940–October 1944
		North Western Europe	October 1944–VE Day
6th	Territorial Army	As 5th HLI	
1/9th (Glasgow Highlanders)	Territorial Army	As 5th HLI	
2/9th (Glasgow Highlanders)	Territorial Army	North Western Europe	June 1944–VE Day
10th	Territorial Army	North Western Europe	June 1944–VE Day
11th	Territorial Army	Converted to Armoured Regiment 1942, later disbanded.	

In addition the 12th and 13th Battalions were employed on home defence duties in the UK and the 14th Battalion was formed in North Africa but never saw active service.

changed from Territorial Force in 1921) makes for an interesting comparison with the 1914 listing printed above.

Among the more obvious changes are the disappearance of cavalry and the conversion of the Glasgow Yeomanry into a regiment of Anti-Tank artillery. The reduction in numbers of infantry battalions is also marked – many Territorial Army infantry battalions were converted to anti-aircraft Regiments in 1938, reflecting the need to combat the threat from the air.

Again mobilisation of the Territorial Army, on 1 September, came just a few weeks after the men's return from annual camp. In 1939 Glasgow's Territorial infantry had been, for their fortnight's annual camp, to Dunfermline (7th Cameronians), Aberdour (5th HLI) and Kinross (6th and 9th HLI), the RAMC units went to Berwick, the Engineers to Irvine while the

80th Field Regiment Royal Artillery went to Redesdale in Northumberland. Other city units travelled as far as Wales for their annual training commitment.

Although the new Territorial Army was designed to operate to the same standards and using the same equipment as the regulars, there were still some obvious problems. Communications were still a problem – the 57th Searchlight Regiment had to appeal in the *Glasgow Herald* on 2 September for twelve civilians with motor cycles to act as voluntary despatch riders. The Territorial Army ceased to exist as a separate entity on 6 September, when it was formally incorporated into the Army.

As in the 1914–18 war Glasgow raised many thousands of men for its own infantry regiment. Mercifully the death rate was lower, but even so the battalions of the HLI lost a total of 104 officers and 1,287 other ranks.

One member of the Regiment, Major Frank G. Blaker, MC, won the Victoria Cross during the Second World War, for an action in Burma in 1944. Major Baker was at the time attached to the 9th Gurkha Rifles.

Fig. 84

Some of the volunteers who would form the 17th (Chamber of Commerce) Battalion of the Highland Light Infantry, lined up outside the Stock Exchange in September 1914. The 17th HLI served on the Western Front in the 32nd Infantry Division – one of Kitchener's New Army Divisions. Also serving in the same division were the other two HLI 'Pals' battalions – the 15th (Tramways) and 16th (Boys Brigade).
(Daily Record)

GLASGOW: A CITY AT WAR

Fig. 85
The trench warfare stalemate of the Western Front called for more and more artillery to give British troops the chance to smash their way through German barbed wire and trenches. Many firms were put to work on the manufacture of artillery and artillery shells. The Cathcart firm of G. & J. Weir, here seen visited by King George V, manufactured 400 trench howitzers as part of this armaments drive.
(Imperial War Museum)

[10]

DOWN TO THE SEA IN SHIPS

Glasgow's wartime connection with the sea was two-fold. The city was of course a great centre of shipbuilding and marine engineering and was also a major focus of the British shipping industry, with a huge infrastructure of quays, docks and anchorages. As a consequence the sea and sea-going were in the blood of the city and many Glaswegians served in the mercantile and Royal navies. The city's long engineering tradition meant that a Glasgow man was to be found in the engine room of many ships on all the oceans of the world, with a clear and well-beaten path leading from an engineering apprenticeship in a shipyard to an engineer's berth on a passenger or cargo vessel. The Royal Navy had learned much of its engineering skills in the nineteenth century by seconding officers to shipyards such as that of Robert Napier at Govan. Indeed, Napier's former 'apprentices' became a significant group of progressive-minded naval officers in the late-Victorian Navy.

The shipyards of Glasgow were a vital part of the nation's defence infra-structure. The range of yards actually located within the city limits was wide – from small specialist yards to the giant yards capable of turning out vessels of very large size.

The Royal Navy's tradition had been to build its ships in the Royal Dockyards: Chatham, Devonport, Portsmouth etc. With steam power and the coming of iron and then steel construction in the mid-nineteenth century this tradition was weakened and shipyards, at first on the Thames and then on the Clyde, developed from being commercial builders to building ships for the Royal Navy. The role of Robert Napier and the Govan yard in this context has been touched on in Chapter 1.

By the years before the First World War Clydeside as a whole was building around a quarter of the Royal Navy's new tonnage and the Glasgow yards were responsible for a very considerable proportion of that.

One highly significant development in the rise of the Clyde to its position as the arsenal for the Royal Navy came in 1906 when Alfred Yarrow moved his yard, which specialised in fast naval vessels (torpedo boat destroyers),

Fig. 90
Fairfield's yard was a major centre of warship building, as it was of commercial building. In any yard much of the success of the enterprise lay in the skilled workforce. This early 1940s photograph shows one of Fairfield's most experienced workers, Willie Rexter, who had survived the loss of the *Titanic* in 1912 and who was a veteran of the Sudanese wars.
(Imperial War Museum)

from Poplar on the Thames to Scotstoun in Glasgow to take advantage of the unique combination of technical education, skills, scientific development, commercial and technical infrastructure that existed on the Clyde. Alfred Yarrow observed at the time: 'When you want apples, you go to Covent Garden; for meat to a meat market, and for ships you go to the north.'

Yarrow's continues in business at Scotstoun to the present day, under the name of BAE Systems, as a specialist naval shipyard with an extensive British and foreign order book, having absorbed the former Blythswood shipyard and the Barclay Curle Elderslie drydocks. In its long and distinguished career the Yarrow yard has produced small naval vessels for countries from Greece and Brazil in the early twentieth century to Malaysia and Brunei in more recent times. They have also continued to turn out destroyers and frigates for the Royal Navy. The company today is the prime contractor for the new Type 45 destroyer for the Royal Navy, the lead ship of the class being due into service in 2007.

Another major specialist warship yard was created on the Clyde in 1905 by William Beardmore & Co Ltd. Although this yard was not located in Glasgow, but downriver at Dalmuir on the western outskirts of Clydebank, it can fairly be considered a Glasgow yard as it was owned and controlled by, and formed an integral part, of the great Glasgow-based Beardmore armaments complex. Although splendidly equipped and very successful in winning Admiralty contracts before and during the First World War, the Dalmuir yard fell victim to the retrenchment and adverse trading conditions of the inter-war period. The international agreement limiting the size and numbers of naval forces – the 1922 Washington Treaty – resulted in the cancellation of a vital battle-cruiser order and the Dalmuir yard eked out its final years building small commercial vessels on berths once destined to build vessels such as the battleship *Ramilies* (1917). It closed in 1930.

Perhaps more durable were the great general yards, among them Fairfield near Govan, which could turn out anything from luxury transatlantic liners such as the *Campania* and *Lucania* of 1893 to the battleships *Valiant* (1916) and *Howe* (1942), the aircraft carrier *Implacable* (1944) and the cruisers *Norfolk* (1930) and *Bellona* (1943).

Other yards, formerly less associated with warship work, such as Alexander Stephen & Sons Ltd at Linthouse on the south bank of the river, also became major suppliers. In the crisis of 1914 the Admiralty needed a rapid expansion of naval shipbuilding capacity and discovered that the Linthouse yard had all the facilities and skills needed to build destroyers, eighteen of which were constructed there during the war period. In the Second World War Stephen & Sons produced, among other Admiralty contracts, the cruisers *Kenya* (1940), *Hermione* (1941) and *Ceylon* (1943), the fast minelayers *Ariadne* (1943) and *Manxsman* (1941), the Tribal class destroyers *Sikh* (1938) and *Zulu* (1938), and the Laforey class destroyers *Matchless* (1941) and *Meteor* (1941). Many of these vessels were part of the immediate pre-war re-armament drive which re-vitalised much of the depressed Clyde shipbuilding industry. Stephen's largest vessel for the Royal Navy was the aircraft carrier *Ocean* (1945). One Linthouse-built sloop, HMS *Amethyst* (1943), found fame after the war when it was at the centre of a confrontation on the Yangtse river with the Chinese Communist Government. *Amethyst* sailed up the Yangtse in April 1949 to protect British citizens caught up in the conflict between the Communist and Nationalist forces. She was fired on and sustained serious damage but eventually made a successful escape – an incident which was filmed as *Yangtze Incident* in 1957.

As significant to the war-effort in both World Wars was the need to repair and refit battle-damaged ships. This was an area in which Stephen of Linthouse also proved to be a major player: in the 1914–18 war, among a great deal of other repair work, they refitted and modified 120 destroyers, 38 minesweepers, 9 cruisers and 10 submarines. In the 1939–45 war, again selecting from a long list of repair contracts, they modified 48 destroyers and refitted and repaired 16 aircraft carriers, 1 battleship and 21 cruisers. The story of one of these cruiser contracts – that of the heavy cruiser *Sussex* – was touched on in Chapter 5.

Crucial as warship-building was in both world wars, the losses, especially from submarine sinkings, of merchant vessels meant that a great effort had to be made to speed up the production of new merchant shipping tonnage, and again Glasgow's yards played a highly significant part in this. In the Second World War Clyde shipyards turned out no fewer than 304 merchant vessels in addition to the huge amount of warship construction, repair and refit work.

Although separate figures for Glasgow yards are not available the Clyde built 1,903 ships, converted 637 others and repaired an astounding 23,191 ships in the six years of the Second World War.

Merchant ships had of course to be adapted and converted to carry defensive armament and although naval parties were sent on board some merchantmen to act as gunners, at least 150,000 merchant service seamen were trained in gunnery during the war.

Many Glasgow-built merchant ships were converted to other roles – as armed merchant cruisers, troopships or assault ships – and of course most of the city's beloved paddle steamers were called up for military service in both wars, serving as minesweepers, convoy escorts, anti-aircraft ships and in other roles. Many paddle steamers were lost in action, for example the *Waverley* (1898) at Dunkirk, while others were found unfit for return to civilian service. The luxury Atlantic liner *Campania*, built at Fairfield's yard in 1892, was dramatically converted to become an aircraft carrier during the First World War and was lost in a collision in November 1918. The much-loved flagship of the Anchor Line, *Columbia*, which sailed from Yorkhill Quay in the heart of the city to New York, was called up for First World War service as an armed merchant cruiser but survived the war to return to her old route. Another Anchor Line ship, *Transylvania*, built by Fairfield in 1925, was requisitioned as an Armed Merchant Cruiser at the start of the war and saw active service. In August 1940 she was torpedoed off Ailsa Craig by *U-56* with the loss of forty-eight lives.

Apart from being a world-class centre of shipbuilding, Glasgow was also home to a disproportionately large number of Britain's shipowning companies. Famous names such as Allan Bros, Burrell & Sons, Paddy Henderson, H. Hogarth & Sons were a few of the many companies which had their origins in Glasgow. As a consequence many of the most notable merchant shipping incidents of both wars involved Glasgow-registered ships. The high level of shipping losses, particularly in the Second World War, naturally affected these companies. The first merchant casualty of the 1939–45 war was the *Athenia*, sunk 200 miles west of the Hebrides on 3 September 1939. *Athenia* was a Glasgow ship in every sense – built at Fairfield's yard in 1922, she was owned by the Glasgow-based Donaldson Line and her regular route was from Glasgow to Canada via Liverpool. She was carrying many Canadian and American passengers returning home because of the outbreak of war; there were also many child evacuees on board. Despite orders to avoid attacking civilian passenger ships, the German submarine *U-33* torpedoed *Athenia* with the loss of 112 lives – an incident which was greeted with a particular horror at the outbreak of war. An investigation was held by the German Navy and the U-boat commander was held to have acted in good faith, believing that the *Athenia* was an armed merchant cruiser rather than an unarmed passenger liner. Indeed Oberleutnant zur See Fritz-Julius Lemp, the commander of the *U-33*, received the Iron Cross on 27 September and was promoted to Kapitänleutnant on 1 October.

Because of the *Athenia's* route and ownership there were, as usual, many Scottish passengers and passengers of Scottish descent on board the vessel.

Another Glasgow-built ship, the tanker *San Demetrio*, launched from the Blythswood Shipyard for the Eagle Oil Company, formed part of a homeward bound convoy from Halifax, Nova Scotia – HX84 – in November

1940. The convoy was attacked by the German pocket battleship *Admiral Scheer* and the convoy escort – the armed merchant cruiser *Jervis Bay* – made a gallant attempt to defend the convoy but was sunk along with five ships from the convoy. Captain Fegan of the *Jervis Bay* won a posthumous VC for his action. The *San Demetrio,* carrying highly flammable aviation fuel, was shelled and seriously damaged. The crew abandoned ship but on the next day seventeen of the crew re-boarded her and extinguished the flames and managed to bring the ship and her vital cargo back to the Clyde.

The Henderson line entered the Second World War with nine ships of the British and Burmese Steam Navigation Company under their management; five of these were lost during the war due to enemy action. During the war Paddy Henderson managed another ten ships for the Ministry of War Transport and three of these were sunk by enemy action and another wrecked. Many of the company's ships were directly involved in military operations and, for example, the Captain, Chief Officer and Chief Engineer of the *Salween* won two Distinguished Service Crosses and an OBE for their role in the evacuation of the British Army from Greece in 1942. Another Paddy Henderson vessel, the *Amarapoora*, was converted into a hospital ship at the outbreak of war, and after service at Scapa Flow was sent in October 1942 to the Mediterranean, where she took part in the Salerno landings in September 1943. After a refit she was sent to the Far East where, among other tasks, she evacuated British POWs and civilian internees from Singapore in August 1945.

The huge loss of vessels and life in the British merchant navy was shared in full measure by Glasgow sailors and shipping lines. Britain and the Empire lost, up to the end of the war in Europe in May 1945, 2,570 ships totalling 11,380,000 gross tons to enemy action. The British merchant navy, despite the huge demands of war and the emergency building programme, ended the Second World War with 15 per cent less tonnage than it had at the outbreak of war – the United States merchant fleet had, on the other hand, grown more than four-fold. Britain's merchant service lost over 35,000 men dead and missing between the outbreak of war and the defeat of Japan in August 1945.

Although Glasgow had an extensive network of docks and harbours, whose contribution to the war effort is discussed in Chapter 12, this was insufficient to sustain the war effort. A huge transfer of dockers and equipment was made from the bomber-vulnerable Thames to the Clyde, and the Clyde Anchorages Emergency Port handled over two million tons of cargo from facilities on the lower river. However a very great deal of this material had to pass through Glasgow for onward shipment by road, rail or sea.

GLASGOW: A CITY AT WAR

The requirements of war at sea had many repercussions on Glasgow. A complex network of naval establishments sprang up in such unlikely places as the St Enoch Station Hotel, which housed an Area Naval Stores Depot and an armaments supply office. Glasgow had its own Admiral, the Flag Officer Glasgow, Vice Admiral Sir J.A.G. Troup, who had been recalled from the retired list to fly his flag in HMS *Spartiate* – which was the Royal Navy's designation for the Glasgow complex of offices centred on the St Enoch Hotel. An admiral could hardly have as his flagship a railway hotel – so for the Navy the hotel became a 'stone frigate'. *Spartiate* had 200 staff when Vice Admiral Troup took up his post but the increasing amount of naval activity relocated to the Clyde from the more vulnerable south coast naval dockyards and bases meant that by the end of the war he had a staff of 600 spread around thirty-six buildings across the city. In addition, an Engineer Rear Admiral ran the Admiralty Regional Office in Glassford Street and a retired commodore was based in the city as Principal Sea Transport Officer (Scottish Ports). There was an RN Victualling Depot at Fordneuk Street in the Gallowgate area and a Gun Mounting Store at Parkhead, among other facilities.

The Sherbrooke Castle Hotel in Pollokshields was converted into a training school, where Merchant Navy radio officers and others were given short but intensive courses in the new technology of radar. So secret was the work that the students were not allowed to take notes for fear that they should fall into enemy hands. When the training school was established radar was still a very scarce tool: the land radar chain had just been completed in time to serve during the Battle of Britain and major naval vessels were beginning to be equipped with radar. For example in May 1941, during the search for the German battleship *Bismarck,* of the two British cruisers patrolling the Denmark Strait only one, HMS *Sheffield,* had up-to-date trainable radar equipment. HMS *Norfolk* had an early version which could only scan a small arc dead ahead; to carry out a sweep the ship, rather than the radar aerial, had to be moved. However as more and more sophisticated sets became available they became fitted to most naval vessels and were also fitted to merchant vessels. It thus became essential to provide a pool of trained operators, and to train merchant service skippers to appreciate the possibilities and limitations of the new device. David Bone, the distinguished sailor/author who ended his career as Sir David Bone, Kt, CBE, LL.D and Commodore of the Anchor Line, was Master of the Fairfield-built cargo/passenger liner *Circassia* during the war. While she was in Glasgow in 1943, being converted into an infantry landing ship and having fourteen assault landing craft mounted on her and all the latest radar and communications equipment installed, Bone was sent to Sherbrooke to have the latest development in radar revealed to him. As he wrote in his engaging book of wartime memories, *Merchantman Rearmed*:

> It was the I.F.F. that brought me up – all standing – to a realisation that I must go to school again and learn at least some rudiment of what seemed a new profession. I.F.F. ('If Friend or Foe') is a small complicated instrument that identifies a distant airplane.

Vice Admiral Troup commented that the Sherbrooke Hotel 'gave a solid contribution to victory at sea'.

Fig. 91

Many visitors came to the Clyde to encourage the war effort (some of these have been discussed in Chapter 6). One who saw something of the work of the city's shipyards was the South African High Commissioner in London, Deneys Reitz (1882–1944), here seen with a riveter at work on a ship for the war programme. Reitz, a former Boer commando, had entered the South African Parliament and became his country's High Commissioner to the UK in 1943. He paid a visit to Glasgow's shipyards and war factories on 7 April 1943, when this photograph was taken, and recalled, at a dinner in the City Chambers, that he had been stationed in the area during the 1914–18 war when he served with the Royal Scots Fusiliers and that he thus felt himself to be on his 'native heath'. *(Imperial War Museum)*

Fig. 92 (top)

One of the ships on which a somewhat younger Willie Rexter (See Fig. 90) might well have worked was HMS *Renown* – a battle-cruiser laid down in January 1915 and completed in September 1916. The battle-cruiser concept was an attempt to produce a ship which could combine the firepower of a battleship with significantly higher speed. This attractive compromise could only be accomplished by reducing the amount of armour protection and thus the overall weight of the ship. *Renown* was capable of five knots, greater speed than contemporary battleships of the *Queen Elizabeth*-class. She served in the Battle Cruiser Squadron of the Grand Fleet in the last two years of the 1914–18 war, but was too late to see action in the major battleship action at Jutland. During the 1939–45 war she had an active record, taking part in the engagement with the German battleships *Scharnhorst* and *Gneisenau* in April 1940, and later operated with Force H from Gibraltar, with the Home Fleet and for the last two years of the war with the Eastern Fleet in action against Japan. She was scrapped in 1948 at Faslane on the Gareloch. *(U.S. Naval Historical Center)*

Fig. 93 (middle)

Fairfield also constructed HMS *Valiant* – a *Queen Elizabeth*-class battleship. *Valiant* was laid down in January 1913, launched in November 1914 and completed in February 1916. She mounted eight 15-inch guns. Like most major units of the fleet she was subject to a number of refits and reconstructions in an attempt to keep her abreast of changing conditions of warfare and new technology. Our photograph dates from after a major refit in 1929–30 and shows her carrying a Fairey III-F floatplane on the quarterdeck. Like *Renown,* her yard-mate and near contemporary, *Valiant* served in the Grand Fleet for the second half of the 1914–18 war. During the 1939–45 war she saw service in almost every theatre, operating off Norway in April 1940 and participating in the Battle of Cape Matapan in the Mediterranean in March 1941. She was damaged by Italian limpet mines in Alexandria harbour in December 1941 but, after repairs, supported the Sicily and Salerno landings in 1943. When conditions in the European theatre of operations ceased to require the presence of so many heavy ships she, like many other major units, was sent to the Far East. *Valiant* was sold for scrapping in March 1948 and was broken up at Cairnryan, Wigtownshire. *(U.S. Naval Historical Center)*

Fig. 94 (below)

The changing nature of war dictated the creation of new types of warship. One of the earliest aircraft carriers was HMS *Argus*, seen here in the Firth of Forth in late 1918 with a paddle-tug alongside. Like all the early aircraft carriers *Argus* was a conversion, in this case of a passenger liner the *Conte Rosso*, which was being built for Italian owners at Beardmore's Dalmuir yard. Other early British carriers such as *Furious* and *Eagle* were based on cruiser or battleship hulls. The first British aircraft carrier to be designed from the start as such was HMS *Hermes,* completed in 1923. Work on *Conte Rosso* was suspended on the outbreak of war and she was purchased on the stocks in 1916 and converted. She became the world's first carrier with a full-length flight deck and became the model for future construction. Her limitations of size and speed restricted her utility but she proved invaluable in training naval aviators. In the Second World War she served with Force H, based at Gibraltar, and her aircraft supported the North African landings. She was scrapped in December 1946 at Inverkeithing, Fife. The dazzle camouflage introduced during the First World War was intended to break up the outline of a ship and make it harder to spot or to target accurately. *(US Naval Historical Center)*

Fig. 95 (above)

Kenya, a Fiji class light cruiser, was laid down at Stephen's Linthouse yard in June 1938, launched in August 1939 and commissioned in August 1940. She mounted twelve 6-inch guns and was capable of 31.5 knots. Her wartime service included participation in the hunt for the *Bismarck,* and involvement in the 'Pedestal' convoy to reinforce Malta (during this engagement she was hit by a torpedo but continued to fight for eight hours to escort the convoy to safety). In April 1943 she was transferred to the Far Eastern Fleet, where she spent the remainder of war. In October 1949 she was again sent to Asian waters and with the outbreak of war in Korea she was involved in supporting the United Nations forces. *Kenya* was broken up at Faslane in 1962. *(Imperial War Museum)*

Fig. 96 (opposite)

The Second World War saw a group of five British battleships come into service. These ships – the King George V class – were started in 1937 and completed between 1940 and 1942. Two of them, *Duke of York* and *Howe,* were built on the Clyde, at John Brown and Fairfield, and this photograph shows the workers leaving *Howe* at the end of the last shift worked on her prior to her leaving the builder's hands. *Howe* and her sister ships mounted ten 14-inch guns and extensive anti-aircraft artillery including 5.25-inch dual purpose guns – a twin mounting of these can be seen behind the workers – a provision that was not sufficient to protect the *Prince of Wales* from being sunk by Japanese naval aircraft in December 1941, along with the battle-cruiser *Repulse. (Imperial War Museum)*

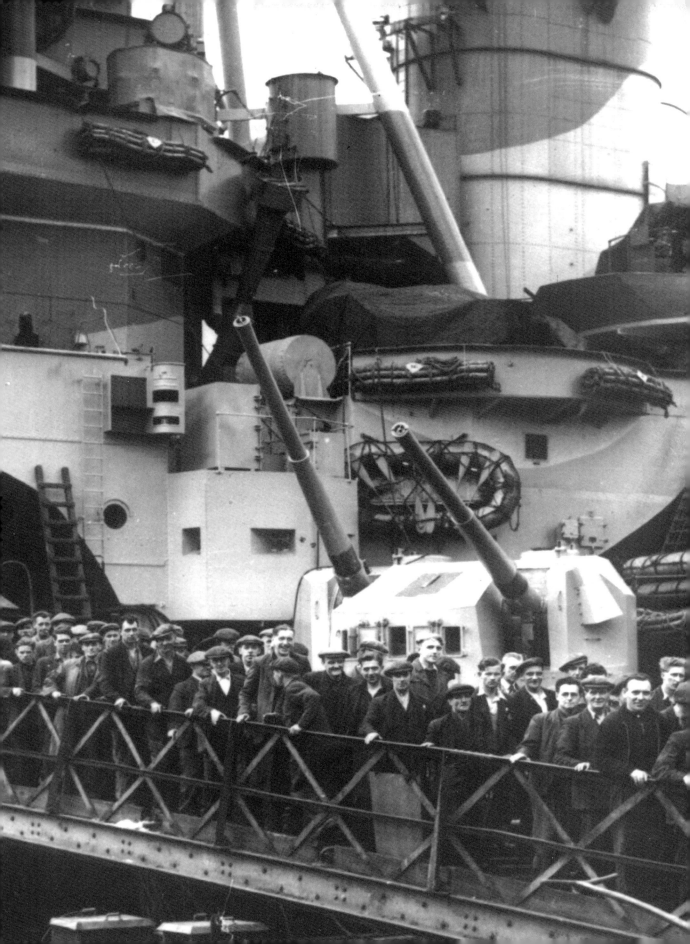

Fig. 97

HMS *Howe* in her
wartime dazzle camouflage
leaving Fairfield's yard at
Govan under the control
of tugs to make her way
down river to join the war.
The photographs shows
the aft X turret of four 14-
inch guns; in the A & B
positions forward were
another four-gun turret
and a two-gun turret.
Howe joined the Home
Fleet and served on the
Arctic convoys to
Murmansk. In 1943 she
was in the Mediterranean
and formed part of the
task force for the invasion
of Sicily. After a refit she
sailed in 1944 to join the
Far East fleet, where she
served for the remainder
of the war. After the war
Howe had a spell as a
training ship and was
broken up at Inverkeithing
in 1958.
(Imperial War Museum)

Fig. 98

In 1937 the Admiralty ordered the Javelin class of destroyers – these 1,700-ton vessels mounted six 4.7-inch guns and ten torpedo tubes. Two of the class were built at Yarrow's – *Jupiter* and *Kipling*. This photograph was taken at *Jupiter's* launch in December 1938. At the beginning of the war she formed part of the 7th Destroyer Flotilla, based at the Nore and engaged on patrol and escort duties. In November 1940 she formed part of the 5th Destroyer Flotilla under Captain Lord Louis Mountbatten and was hit by two torpedoes while operating out of Plymouth. After a brief spell in the Mediterranean *Jupiter* was sent to the Far East and had an active career against Japanese forces before being sunk in the Battle of the Java Sea. The combined Australian, British, Dutch and American force of five cruisers and nine destroyers encountered a Japanese force of two heavy and two light cruisers and fourteen destroyers. *Jupiter* hit a mine, thought to have been laid earlier that day by an Allied vessel. Ninety-seven of the survivors, including the Captain, Lt Commander Thew, were captured by the Japanese, and twenty-seven of them died in captivity. *(BAE Systems)*

Fig. 99 (above)

Oakley was a Hunt class escort destroyer, one of a large class of vessels designed to meet the Royal Navy's requirement to provide convoy escorts which were cheap to build and run. She was built at Yarrow's Scotstoun yard, was launched in January 1942 and completed in May of that year. The Hunt class destroyers were costed at £400,000 each, compared to the £610,000 price of the Javelin class ships. *Oakley* was one of the Type 2 Hunts, with increased armament and larger dimensions, four of which were built by Yarrow's. Although the Hunt class had insufficient range for use on Atlantic convoys they proved to be successful in the North Sea and Mediterranean. After *Oakley's* Royal Navy service she was transferred to the West German Navy where she was named *Gneisenau*. *(BAE Systems)*

Fig. 100 (below)

The many areas in which the Royal Navy operated had their own special requirements and HMS *Locust* was a river gunboat, which might have normally been expected to operate in the Far East. Ordered under the 1938 Estimates she was launched in 1940 from Yarrow's Scotstoun yard and found herself in a variety of roles including supporting the Dieppe raid in August 1942 where her shallow draft and armament of two 4-inch guns and a 3.7-inch howitzer could be put to good use. After her wartime service *Locust* became an RNVR drill ship in 1951. *(BAE Systems)*

Fig. 101 (above)

The Sherbrooke Hotel, together with a number of adjacent houses, was requisitioned for service as a radar training school and many deck and radio officers of the Merchant Navy were trained in the use and operation of radar apparatus at this Pollokshields establishment. This photograph shows five of the permanent staff of WRENS who worked at the establishment. In the left background can be seen the distinctive high square tower of the hotel – which made an excellent site for the radar scanner. *(Mrs Betty Gray)*

Fig. 102 (opposite)

HMS *Aristocrat*, seen here with her electrical officer Sub Lt. A. Mitchell, RNVR, playing the pipes as she sails for the Normandy landings in June 1944, was a very familiar sight to Glaswegians in its civilian guise as the DEPV *Talisman* – built in 1935 at A. & J. Inglis Pointhouse yard beside the River Kelvin for the LNER's route from Craigendoran to Rothesay. In 1940 she was requisitioned for war service and equipped as an anti-aircraft ship. During the war she saw service as far afield as North Africa, where she was involved in the Allied landings. In the D-Day landings on the Normandy coast she acted as the HQ ship for the Mulberry harbours. After the war she returned to the Clyde to serve the Craigendoran to Kirn and Dunoon route. She was broken up at Dalmuir in 1967. *(Imperial War Museum)*

Fig. 103 (above)

When a warship finally leaves the builder's hands it is formally commissioned into the Royal Navy in an impressive service. This photograph shows the first draft of what would at full strength be the 2,000-strong crew of the new fleet carrier HMS *Implacable* lined up on the flight deck to take part in her commissioning. She was launched at Fairfield's Govan yard in December 1942 and completed in August 1944. The 23,000-ton displacement *Implacable* took four and a half years to complete from her laying down in February 1939, but work on her was suspended in 1940 and her completion was treated as a low priority matter. After a few months' service with the Home Fleet she was transferred to the British Pacific Fleet in March 1945 and took part in operations against Japan. Employed in a training role from 1946 to 1949 she was again an operational carrier in 1952–54 and was paid off in August 1954 and broken up in November 1955. Her short life was due to her inability to operate the larger modern aircraft which came into service late in the war and after the war. *(Imperial War Museum)*

Fig. 104 (opposite)

Many of Glasgow's steamers were commissioned for service during both world wars. This picture shows the Fairfield-built paddle steamer *Jupiter* which was called up in 1939 to serve as a minesweeper and in 1941 became an anti-aircraft vessel and served in the Thames and at the Normandy landings. Because there already was an HMS *Jupiter* (see Fig. 98) in Royal Navy service the paddler was renamed HMS *Scawfell*. She returned to civilian service after the war and sailed Clyde routes until 1957. She was broken up at Dublin in 1961.
(Imperial War Museum)

[11]

THE DEFENCE INDUSTRIES

Glasgow had long had some record as a centre of war production. During the Napoleonic Wars, carronades, the short-barrelled, short-range cannon which had been invented in the 1770s at the Carron Iron Works near Falkirk, were being cast at the Clyde Iron Works in the east of the city and were sent down river to Dumbarton to be finished at the works of James and John Napier. However, in general, the city, shipbuilding excepted, was not really seen as a significant centre of munitions and arms supply.

This situation changed at the end of the nineteenth century with the rise to prominence as a centre of defence production of the Parkhead Forge, owned and run by William Beardmore. Parkhead had long been in the Beardmore family's hands but William brought both scientific training and managerial flair to it. Parkhead became an integral part of a major armaments complex. In the pre-1914 naval armaments race the Beardmore companies could offer an integrated production of ships, armoured plate and guns. As part of this ambitious scheme Beardmore, who had bought the old Robert Napier shipyard at Govan (see *Black Prince* Chapter 1), realising that the situation of the Govan yard was not ideal and recognising the advantages of a modern, purpose-built yard incorporating all the latest technological advances, built a new battleship yard downriver at Dalmuir. During the First World War this part of the Beardmore empire diversified into aircraft, artillery and tank production.

While Beardmore was essentially an armaments firm other local defence suppliers were often firms which had been founded to meet specific civilian needs and which became involved in military work as a response to wartime pressures.

There was of course a problem in this – much of the industrial effort of Glasgow and Clydeside was heavily committed to shipbuilding and it was not easy to identify engineering capacity and labour which could be devoted to other war purposes, for example meeting the unprecedented demand for munitions, particularly artillery shells, created by the trench warfare stalemate on the Western Front.

One of the ways in which this problem was solved was by using many small concerns, even garages and bicycle repair shops, to produce shell

Fig. 105

The First World War saw a vast increase in military aviation and the existing aircraft manufacturing capacity of the country was quite inadequate to meet the demand. The Royal Aircraft Factory (later the Royal Aircraft Establishment) at Farnborough sub-contracted construction to a wide range of companies from piano makers to established engineering firms like Weirs of Cathcart who became the first Clyde firm to receive an order for the BE 2c single-engine two-seater fighter bi-plane. Weir built 300 of this model, as well as 386 FE 2b and 450 DH9 aircraft. This photograph shows part of the production line and is an interesting reminder of the very small size of First World War fighter aircraft. *(The Weir Group)*

components. The labour shortage was tackled by the process of 'dilution'. This involved bringing in unskilled workers to tackle the less demanding part of various jobs – leaving the time-served skilled workers to perform only the more exacting elements. It also, and equally controversially, involved the employment of women workers. Prior to the First World War there had been only a very tiny number of women employed in the metal industries of Clydeside – some 3,700 women against 185,000 men. The largest single group of these women was in the Singer Manufacturing Company, making sewing machines at Clydebank. By June 1916 18,500 women were employed in the metal trades in the Clyde district and around half of the munitions workers were women. This female labour came from near and far – one Glasgow factory engaged on war work hired 200 fisher-women from the Outer Hebrides.

This so-called dilution process was often fiercely resisted by the trade unions, anxious to protect hard-won positions and differentials. In many cases the resistance to dilution was carried forward by unofficial groups of workers. As mentioned earlier, even so charismatic a speaker as David Lloyd George, the Minister of Munitions, found the Clyde workers a singularly resistant audience when he came to Glasgow to make the case for dilution in December 1915 (see Chapter 3).

The war also greatly increased demand for textiles for uniforms, chemicals for explosives, electrical generating and lighting equipment for army camps, and agricultural engineering equipment to mechanise farms to compensate for the loss of manpower and to reduce reliance on imported foods.

Some well-known Glasgow companies found the nature of their business radically changed by the exigencies of war. George and James Weir set up a machine shop, smithy and foundry in Cathcart in 1886 and soon built up a successful business supplying pumps and other ancillary equipment to the developing steamship industry. In the 1914–18 war, under the control of James Weir's son, William Douglas Weir, the Cathcart works vastly expanded with two new factories, Albert (named after the King of the Belgians) and Flanders (named after the focus of much of the fighting on the Western Front) being created for the production of shells.

When the company decided to build these new factories they did so in response to the national crisis and declared that:

> … all profits arising from the manufacture of Shell under present contracts, after deduction of necessary allowances for establishment charges and capital expenditure, shall be handed over to certain of the various organisations carrying out relief work or Red Cross work which the war has necessitated …

Unfortunately labour relations were such that the workforce, concerned about changes in working practices and the dilution of skilled trades by unskilled workers and women workers were convinced that the employers were operating a hidden agenda. In their turn the directors of the company were incensed that the workers were not echoing their patriotic gesture. A widespread Clyde engineering strike in February/March 1915 did much to create the reputation of 'Red Clydeside.'

Shell production at the Albert Factory, which had peaked at 3,500 8-inch shells a week, ceased in 1917 and the equipment was transferred to the new National Projectile Factory at nearby Cardonald. The Flanders plant produced 6,000 6-inch shells per week, and also turned out great quantities of smaller calibre munitions. The Albert was turned over to aircraft production and over 1,100 aircraft were produced at Cathcart during the war, with Weir's becoming the Clyde area's largest aircraft manufacturer.

The wartime shipbuilding boom obviously created an increased demand for the company's core products and in addition the works turned out artillery pieces for the army and a wide range of other war material, far removed from their core pump and auxiliary machinery business. At their wartime peak Weir's employed over 6,000 employees, including 2,000 women.

The technical and administrative abilities of William Douglas Weir meant that he was quickly picked up by the Government and, in 1915, he was made Controller of Aeronautical Supplies at the Ministry of Munitions. Created Baron Weir in 1918 he became Secretary of State for Air in Lloyd George's cabinet and played a major role in uniting the Royal Flying Corps and the Royal Naval Air Service into the Royal Air Force.

The needs of war meant that many companies had to move away from their traditional specialisations, either partially or totally. An excellent local example of this was the North British Locomotive Company at Springburn. While demand for railway locomotives did not stop during the First or Second World War – indeed there were major military railways created behind the Western Front in the 1914–18 war – the engineering facilities and skilled personnel at Springburn were diverted to other, more urgent, war work.

Two new buildings which were in construction at the outbreak of war were completed and re-christened the Mons and Marne factories (named after the battles of August 1914 and September 1914) and devoted initially to the production of 8-inch shells. The Mons factory was from the first entirely staffed by women, with the exception of the foremen, tool setters and machine repair departments. The Mons workforce peaked at 1,136 women and 405 men in October 1918. Over 146,000 8-inch shells were produced before production shifted to the shells for the 18-pounder field gun and the 6-inch gun and howitzer. Over 387,000 18-pounder shells were produced.

Springburn further diversified into the production of torpedo tubes – these had previously been manufactured in the Royal Dockyards and supplied to shipbuilders, but the increased demand of wartime production had overstretched the resources of the Royal Dockyards and recourse was made to private contractors such as North British Loco.

The tank, the new weapon, designed to break the stalemate on the Western Front, was also manufactured at Springburn and 100 'Medium B' tanks and 1,040 'Mark VIII' tanks were ordered from the North British Locomotive Company.

During the Second World War Springburn again turned its plant to the manufacture of tanks, completing a contract for 143 light tanks in 1940 and then moving over to the production of the 26-ton Matilda tank – a vehicle designed essentially as an infantry support weapon. Over 600 Matildas were built at Springburn before it was decided that the demand for locomotives constituted a higher priority for the Springburn plant and tank production ceased. In 1942 the Ministry of Supply ordered the production of the Austerity WD 2-8-0 locomotive. The urgency of the order meant that drawings were produced and production materials ordered within sixteen days of the order being placed and the first of 545 of the Austerity model were delivered within five months of the order date.

Apart from locomotives and tanks, Springburn produced 1.6 million bombs and shells during the 1939–45 war as well as 13,000 mines and, perhaps more unexpectedly, 800 dough-mixing bowls for the Royal Navy.

An important specialised defence contractor in Glasgow was the firm of Barr & Stroud, which became the major supplier of optical instruments such as rangefinders, heightfinders, gun-sights, bomb-sights, periscopes and field glasses to British and foreign armed forces. Their Anniesland factory was a prime target for German bombers, but escaped damage during the Clydeside air-raids.

In the pre-Second World War period one advantage that Glasgow had was its geographical situation: it enjoyed a certain degree of safety from bombing attacks – at least as compared to the more vulnerable factories in the London area and the Midlands. The government, acting on the recommendations of a panel of expert advisers, headed by Lord Weir, introduced a policy to encourage the building of Shadow Factories for the defence industries.

Rolls Royce built a plant at Crewe to manufacture their new Merlin engine and then planned a further, and much larger aero-engine plant at Glasgow. This factory was designed to take advantage of Glasgow's remoteness from German airfields and the area's reserves of manpower and skills base. In 1939 work started on the £4 million plant on a greenfield site at the Hillington

Industrial Estate. Hillington was planned to be the largest aero-engine establishment in the world with a planned workforce, when full production was achieved, of 10,000. It would be six times larger than Rolls Royce's Crewe factory.

The Merlin engine, which was turned out in huge quantities at Derby, Crewe and Hillington – a total of 168,040 in all its various models and marks was eventually achieved – was one of the great success stories of the Second World War and a genuine war-winning device. It powered Hurricane, Spitfire, Kittyhawk and Mustang fighters, Mosquito and Beaufighter fighter-bombers, Halifax, Whitley, Wellington and Lancaster bombers and various other types.

During the Second World War J. & G. Weir again diversified from their core businesses and, using the spare space created in the First World War, became a 'shadow' factory, concentrating on the manufacture of field artillery. The British Army had produced a specification for a new 25-pounder field gun, and a production design was confirmed in December 1938. Weir's produced the gun carriage and recoil system and bought in other components for final assembly. By the end of 1943 they had built over 3,500 gun carriages, about a third of the army's total requirements and were substantially the largest manufacturer of this equipment. Weir's were also involved in the production of the 6-pounder anti-tank gun.

Fig. 106

The 4-inch naval gun was a standard weapon during the First World War and was fitted as main armament to destroyers and other escort vessels and as secondary armament on cruisers and battleships. The Beardmore armaments complex at Parkhead Forge in the East End of Glasgow and the Dalmuir shipyard downriver were major suppliers of guns of all types. This photograph shows a week's production. *(Glasgow University Archives)*

GLASGOW: A CITY AT WAR

Fig. 107 (below)

The high demand for shell, which far outstripped the resources of the traditional armaments manufacturers, meant that many other companies which had facilities that could be adapted for armaments work were pressed into service. This photograph shows a shell production line at the North British Locomotive Works – note that the workforce is female. *(Mitchell Library NB Loco Collections)*

Fig. 108 (above)

Professor Archibald Barr and Dr William Stroud established a company in Glasgow in 1888 and built up a world-wide reputation in the field of optics. The construction of range-finders for military and naval use became the major part of their business and this 1914 photograph shows, in the foreground, a 9-foot FQ naval rangefinder – this model had gone into production in 1906 and was fitted to battleships in Britain and many foreign countries. In the background, on the workbenches, are 15-foot base FT naval rangefinders. As the importance of aircraft increased the company also produced heightfinders – one of which appears in Fig. 28.
(Thales Optronics)

Fig. 109 (top)
North British Locomotive's first tank contract of the Second World War was for 143 light tanks. This contract was completed by 1940 and production then switched over to the much heavier Matilda tank. This 26-ton vehicle was designed as an 'Infantry Tank', that is, a heavily armoured tank which sacrificed speed to protection, and was intended to give close support to infantry units. A pre-war model, the Mark I, had only been fitted with machine guns but proved too vulnerable to enemy armour. The Mark II was fitted with a 2 lb 40mm anti-tank cannon and saw service from France in May 1940 to the Far East in 1945. *(Mitchell Library NB Loco Collection)*

Fig. 110 (above)
Although North British Locomotive built about one fifth of the total production of Matilda II, the decision was made to allow the works to revert to its basic role as a locomotive builder. This had never entirely ceased and this photograph shows a Matilda at Springburn alongside a Springburn-built locomotive. It will be noticed that the gun has still to be fitted to the tank chassis. *(Mitchell Library NB Loco Collection)*

Fig. 111 (above)

One of the problems facing the Allied forces when they landed in Normandy in June 1944 was that they would be faced with ever-lengthening long lines of supply as they advanced through France, Belgium, the Netherlands and into Germany. It could be expected that the retreating Germans would take steps to deny the Allies use of the major Channel ports. While road transport would be central to the supply requirements of the Allied armies, rail would have its part to play. However, the rail networks and rolling stock of France had been priority targets for the Allied Air Forces in the pre-invasion period. In consequence not only was a major reconstruction of rail infrastructure needed but rolling stock was also required. Our photograph shows NB Loco 78250 being shipped over to France on a Landing Craft (Tank).
(Mitchell Library NB Loco Collection)

Fig. 112 (opposite)

One of the 619 Matildas built at Springburn being lowered into a water tank to test its hull's integrity. The Matilda soon became outclassed by German tanks and anti-tank guns and its slow speed and short range proved to be limitations in the North African desert war.
(Mitchell Library NB Loco Collection)

Fig. 113

The first British bomber to fly a mission over Germany in the Second World War was a Blenheim Mk IV, which carried a total bomb load of two 500-lb semi-armour piercing bombs. By the end of the war modified Lancasters were carrying the 12,000-lb 'Tallboy' and 22,000-lb 'Grand Slam' earthquake bombs designed by Dr Barnes Wallis. The monster bombs were designed to be dropped from a great height, develop supersonic speed on their descent due to their spin and aerodynamic profile and penetrate targets such as reinforced concrete U-boat pens. The 'Tallboy' was used to sink the German battleship *Tirpitz*. This August 1944 photograph shows a pattern for a large bomb at the North British Locomotive Works, with an employee positioned alongside for scale. Presumably the traditional practice of engineering works photographs was adhered to – find the smallest man in the factory and so make the product look larger! *(Mitchell Library NB Loco Collection)*

Fig. 114 (opposite)

The Rolls Royce Merlin engine was one of the undoubted war-winning devices. Fitted to a huge range of aircraft from fighters to heavy bombers it was manufactured at a number of Rolls Royce plants but the Hillington factory built, overhauled and repaired more than 50,000 Merlin engines. Women workers were extensively employed at Hillington and this photograph shows some of them at work on Merlin cylinder blocks. *(Rolls Royce Heritage Trust)*

Fig. 115

The size of the specially built aero-engine works built from 1939 onwards at Hillington on the south-western fringes of Glasgow is very clearly conveyed in this aerial photograph. Hillington was well known to the German air force and figured in their aerial reconnaissance photographs but in the bombing raids of 1941 the Luftwaffe concentrated on targets along the Clyde. *(Rolls Royce Heritage Trust)*

[12]

ON THE OFFENSIVE

Fig. 116

During the Second World War, the River Clyde and its firth had a profound and complex impact on the wider global conflict through, for example, shipbuilding, convoys and strategic shipping movements associated with the Battle of the Atlantic. In October 1942, however, the port of Glasgow itself was suddenly thrust centre-stage at a crucial juncture in the conduct of the war. The city's role changed from providing mainly defensive responses to Axis power, to a direct and intimate involvement in the Allies' plans for seizing the initiative and beginning to fight back. Glasgow had a vital role in the planning and preparation of a series of large-scale land and sea operations. These changed the course of history, and, as the codename of the first of them – Operation *Torch* – suggests, brought the flame of freedom to occupied areas.

Torch was the important offensive of 8 November 1942 that led to the Anglo–US landings at Algiers and elsewhere on the North African coast. The lynchpin of the whole operation was a Glasgow dock on the south side of the River Clyde. The loading of British and American troops onto ships for the *Torch* convoys (and subsequent operations) took place not only at the Tail of the Bank and in the Gareloch, but also, crucially, upriver at the King George V Dock; 'KG5' was Glasgow's military embarkation point and a hive of activity both night and day. In conditions of the utmost security long troop-trains jammed with Allied troops and a wide diversity of units and special forces pulled into the loops of railway that surrounded the dock and unloaded their passengers into the long embarkation sheds. From there the men transferred to the troop transports that lined the long docksides; up to ten ships of this type could be accommodated at KG5 but aircraft carriers, convoy escort vessels and armed merchantmen also made use of the facility. Unlike other docks on the Clyde, KG5 had just one huge basin that enabled large ships to manoeuvre easily into berths along either side of the dock. This was a brilliantly simple arrangement described by David W. Bone in his very fine 1949 memoir as the:

Fig. 116

This photograph from the Clyde Port Authority shows the King George V Dock a few years after the First World War, at a time when the dock's wartime characteristics were still evident. The railway tracks and the long embarkation sheds running along both sides of the giant dock are still clearly visible – it was here that the long trains carrying troops under conditions of the greatest secrecy would arrive to load the waiting troop transports moored along the long docksides. The presence of a dredger reminds us of the necessity to keep the channel clear so that large vessels could come close to the heart of Glasgow.

(Clydeport Archive)

GLASGOW: A CITY AT WAR

Military Embarkation Dock at which troops were marched on board ship up a long sloping gangway (or brow) whose other end might ultimately rest on Norway, Africa, India, Burma or Australia, wherever the fortune of the day required them. It is sufficiently remote from the city and public observation of troop movements. A network of railway lines flows into it on the western side and it was generally in darkness the long troop trains drew into or hauled out from the dockside halt on rail connection with all parts of the Kingdom.
David W. Bone, Merchantman at War

Captain Bone gives a vivid account of the involvement in *Torch* of the vessel under his command, which, as previously mentioned, was the Anchor Line passenger-cargo liner *Circassia*, built at Fairfield's in 1937 as a passenger-cargo liner and now commissioned as an armed merchant cruiser. *Circassia* formed part of the task-force from the Clyde to North Africa, and joined the force at KG5. The transports then made their way down-river and rendezvoused with the larger transports from the Clyde Task Force, and from the Eastern Task Force from Northern Ireland, in the outer Firth of Clyde before beginning their long voyage. The build-up to *Torch* was the biggest assemblage of troopships and other transports ever seen on the Clyde, totalling almost 300 ships.

Circassia was a member of what was described in the sealed orders as the Second Fast Convoy – objective the seaport of Algiers. At about the same time, other parts of the Mediterranean assault force were landing at Oran, while the US task force targeted Casablanca and elsewhere on the Atlantic coast of Morocco. *Circassia* and other Clyde-based transports made several further round trips to the Mediterranean as the African campaign progressed.

Something of the same excitement and importance can be felt in Bone's account of the build-up to the next major offensive. This was Operation *Husky*, the Allied invasion of Sicily (striking at the enemy's 'soft underbelly', to use Churchill's graphic, if not entirely accurate phrase) from North Africa on 10 July 1943. Again a crucial part of the plan involved Glasgow's port and again KG5 was a fulcrum for the build-up of the multi-national force. *Circassia* on this occasion was taken to Yorkhill Basin in Glasgow to be completely reconditioned and converted to what was in the official parlance known as a Landing Ship, Infantry (Large). She was to carry commandos and a flotilla of fourteen Assault Landing Craft. The ALCs were square-ended and flat-bottomed boats, twin-engined and capable of a speed of six or seven knots. They were over forty feet long and carried around thirty-five soldiers and their gear, together with three crew. The landing craft were to be slung from special davits, seven a side and double-banked one above the other. The target area for the Clyde part of the force was a bay on the south-east coast of the island of Sicily. Here the landing craft, their troops and crews reaped their reward after the long weeks of training, practising offshore landings on the more familiar beaches of Brodick, Lamlash, Inveraray and Loch Fyne.

And so to the ultimate maritime campaign in Europe, Operation *Overlord*, D-Day and the Normandy landings. In this instance the Clyde was of course only one component of an immense enterprise, but even so KG5 still had a vital part to play. Hundreds of thousands of GIs and Canadians continued to stream across the Atlantic in troop transports like the Clyde's own 'Queens'. At the Tail of the Bank many were then transferred to other vessels via KG5 – the Glasgow dock was also a clearing house for immense quantities of supplies, including weaponry, transports and much more.

The voyage of a US-built aircraft carrier is evidence of this. Under the terms of the Lend Lease Scheme, the Royal Navy acquired HMS *Puncher* – an auxiliary carrier originally named USS *Willapa*. She came across the North Atlantic in early 1944, acting as an escort for Convoy CU-38, as part of the build-up to the Allies' landings on the Atlantic seaboard. The carrier was heavily loaded with (mainly) fighter aircraft lashed down on the flight-deck, in addition to her own complement of planes and vital military stores. *Puncher* reached KG5, berthed, and immediately began unloading – now ready to fulfil her role as a strike carrier, to use the US classification.

In a similar fashion, even before the entry of the US into the war, large quantities of smaller aircraft such as fighters and fighter-bombers had been crated or secured on the decks of cargo vessels and shipped to the Clyde and upriver to Glasgow. They were brought into King George V Dock then taken by road to Abbotsinch airfield where they were assembled before being flown on elsewhere. This was the transatlantic route for many aircraft, but increasingly as the US build-up gathered momentum, the giant Prestwick airbase became the focal point. Prestwick was the base – to an extent largely unknown at the time – used for ferrying to Europe huge numbers of strategic bombers like Flying Fortresses in what was known as the Atlantic Bridge. Chapter 7 discusses more on the significance of the city of Glasgow in relation to air power.

As already mentioned, security was an obsession, but one that seems justified in retrospect. Ships arriving in the Clyde displayed for their crews a poster that hammered home certain key points:

ON ARRIVAL

Do not talk about the ship or whence she sailed or when. Do not say what ships were seen on the voyage.

Only tell your friends of incidents within the ship in your letters and do not mention the name of the ship.

Never give away the names or descriptions of other ships in company or of friendly aircraft that may have been seen.

Tittle tattle, idle gossip, and giving credence to rumours may endanger the vessel in which you have now so many friends.

GLASGOW: A CITY AT WAR

At later stages in the war, Glasgow was deeply involved in the movement and equipping of the armada of sea-borne forces assembled in support of Operation *Overlord* and the Normandy landings. Into Glasgow were shipped sections of the ingenious 'Mulberry Harbours' – a key part of the master plan for invasion. These had been assembled in Lanarkshire and transported or towed by ships from Glasgow. Commodore Hughes-Hallett, who had commanded the joint services establishment at Inveraray, was credited with the original idea of a 'Mulberry Harbour', which Winston Churchill described as:

> A large area of sheltered water protected by a breakwater based on blockships brought to the scene by their own power and then sunk in a prearranged position.

So the concept of the floating harbour was established, but became increasingly elaborate and sophisticated:

> The whole project was majestic. On the beaches themselves would be the great piers, with their seaward ends afloat and sheltered. At these piers coasters and landing-craft would be able to discharge at all states of the tide. To protect them against the wanton winds and waves breakwaters would be spread in a great arc to seaward, enclosing a large area of sheltered water.

When June 1944 arrived, these two fabricated artificial harbours (one for US and one for British/Canadian forces) did indeed provide shelter for the huge fleet of support vessels bringing men and supplies across the Channel, until Allied forces could break out from the beaches. As mentioned in another chapter the Glasgow-built paddle steamer *Talisman* (or HMS *Aristocrat* to use her wartime name) was one of many Clyde-built ships already at work in the English Channel. She now saw service as a headquarters ship for the Mulberry Harbours. Rear Admiral H. Hickling, CBE, DSO, who had charge of the construction of the harbour on the Normandy beaches, went on record:

> The whole success of the invasion depended on the 'Mulberry' and without it they could have had no guarantee that the vital supplies for our armed forces could have been landed.

Both strategically and logistically, Glasgow and the Clyde were at the heart of the Allies' response to the Axis powers' occupation of Fortress Europe – in three major operations and in numerous other joint military and naval campaigns their workforce and other personnel made a remarkable contribution.

Fig. 117

A low-angle view of the King George V Dock during the Second World War shows a number of transports and other naval vessels in their berths – most are pointing into the dock, as in Fig. 116. In this rarely-seen photograph, one of the tugs that will tow the loaded troopships out into the river is seen manoeuvring close to a large warship and a hospital ship. On the opposite side of the dock is an aircraft carrier pointing outwards to the opening into the dock. From KG5 Dock sailed many of the ships that made up the convoy for Operation *Torch*, bound for North Africa and a major step in the counter attacks against the Axis Powers in October 1942. *(Clydeport Archive)*

Fig. 118

Every picture tells a story but few are more interesting than this First World War photograph. It is a view of P. S. *Waverley*, in the process of passing a mine sweep in collaboration with another paddle steamer, *Lady Moyra*. The photograph is undated, but both vessels were requisitioned by the Admiralty in 1915 and served through the remainder of the war as minesweepers. *Waverley* (the ship which appears bow on), was the third steamer to bear that name and was built in Glasgow in 1899 at the yard of A. & J. Inglis of Pointhouse – the largest Clyde steamer ever to sail under the colours of the North British Steam Packet Company. The *Lady Moyra* was a product of John Brown's of Clydebank, launched in 1905 for the Barry Railway Company, under the name *Gwalia* and re-named on her sale to the Furness Railway Company in 1910 for use on the Barrow to Fleetwood service. So both were Clydebuilt, and the resemblances did not end there: they entered Admiralty service at almost the same time, *Waverley*, as can be seen, bearing the pendant no. 932, and the *Lady Moyra* 937. The apparatus on the latter vessel's deck is the paravane, an invention that greatly increased the efficiency of minesweepers. Both were requisitioned again in the Second World War, undertaking varied duties in 1939; then – final coincidence – they were both lost in action, bombed and sunk at Dunkirk in June 1940, two of the 235 vessels lost in the evacuation of the British Expeditionary Force. *(Imperial War Museum)*

Fig. 119

Following the entry of the USA into the war in late 1941 US warships began to be seen in the Clyde. This vessel is the aircraft carrier USS *Wasp* and may possibly be the same carrier as seen in Fig. 117. The *Wasp* was part of a British–US force sent to the Mediterranean with up to eighty Hurricane aircraft to assist in the defence of Malta. *Wasp* was later sunk in the Western Pacific.

Fig. 120 (above)

The diesel-engined Clyde steamer *Talisman*, (see also Fig. 102) is seen in her wartime garb as HMS *Aristocrat*. She served as a key command ship in the Normandy landings, having earlier sailed from the Clyde to the Mediterranean as part of Operation *Torch*. The *Talisman* was built in 1935, also by A. & J. Inglis. *(Imperial War Museum)*

Fig. 121 (opposite)

Mulberry pier-heads photographed in 1944 off Selsey Bill in the English Channel. This shows the great masterplan that was the Mulberry concept, nearing completion in preparation for D-Day. Out of a total of twenty-three pier-heads, eighteen were constructed at the Parkneuk Works in Motherwell and taken via the port of Glasgow to the south coast. When June 1944 arrived, these vast fabricated artificial harbours provided shelter for the huge invasion fleet making for the Normandy beaches as part of Operation *Overlord*. *(Imperial War Museum)*

Fig. 122

A US Lockheed P-80 Shooting Star fighter is seen being unloaded from the USS *Barney Kirschbaum* at Glasgow's KG5 Dock. The photograph would appear to date from the very late stages of the Second World War, because it is known that this particular ship was laid up before the end of 1945. The *Barney Kirschbaum* is an example of one of the remarkable mass-produced Liberty ships, in this instance being delivered on 13 April 1945, only two months after her keel was laid in Panama City, Florida on 15 February. A number of USAF personnel can be seen on deck together with (presumably) welcoming British officials and a film cameraman. The Shooting Star was a fighter/fighter-bomber/recon-naissance plane – the first USAF aircraft to exceed 500 mph in level flight, the first American jet aircraft to be manufactured in large quantities and the first USAF jet to be used in combat. This example being winched from the ship's hold is one of several sent to Europe for demonstration, but the war ended before the aircraft could be employed in combat. As a postscript – on 8 November, 1950, a later version – an F-80C flown by Lt Russell J. Brown – flying with the 16th Fighter-Interceptor Squadron, shot down a Russian-built MiG-15 in the world's first all-jet fighter air battle.
(The Mitchell Library)

[13]

AFTER THE WARS ARE OVER

Neil Munro's humorous character Erchie appeared for the first time in the columns of the *Glasgow Evening News* in February 1902. In a typically satirical look at current events, Erchie anticipates the end of the Boer War at the Treaty of Vereeniging by a number of weeks:

> The war's feenished. Jist gaed oot in a flaff like a' thae kin' o' things. Arteelery, horse, fit and Marines, the British Airmy's on its way hame … I hinna heard yet whether they jist smashed a' the Boers to the fore, or spread bird-lime on the veldt and catched them by the feet, or cam' away leavin' the puir craturs wi' nae mair chance o' getting khaki clothes and convoy ammunition and rations; but the thing's shair that they're comin' hame onyway.

This informative if jocular retrospective glance at military matters was prompted by some purely local political manoeuvres (the returning soldiery was rumoured to be applying in large numbers for the job of Glasgow's Chief Constable). It does, however, raise the age-old problem of what happens when wars come to an end and there is a sudden precipitation of large numbers of men onto the job market. Later in the twentieth century Glasgow's arrangements were tested to the limit in the wake of not one but two world wars.

First of all, though, there were the jubilant victory celebrations, as described in the columns of the *Glasgow Herald* in 1918:

> The end of the greatest war in history was celebrated with enthusiasm throughout the country. It was the greatest day of rejoicing Glasgow has ever known … The scenes witnessed in Sauchiehall Street, Renfield Street, and other central thoroughfares were not less arresting to the observant eye than those in Buchanan Street. Everywhere was bunting, flags, bannerets, and lines of streamers. Rejoicing groups of lads, munition workers, warehouse

Fig. 123
The end of the Second World War is marked officially in Glasgow by a Victory Parade in George Square, watched by a huge crowd. Over 3,000 men and women of the three fighting services took part, together with detachments of the United States Army, the Polish Army, the Home Guard, and various non-combatant and junior organisations including scouts, guides and cadets. Another junior organisation represented in the celebrations were the Foundry Boys – a Victorian youth organisation devoted to the religious, moral and physical improvement of the lot of Glasgow children. Originally concerned with, as the title suggests, boys working in the foundry trades, the society's activities later widened into other employment areas and to work with girls.
(The Daily Record)

people, shopkeepers – for most of the places of business closed early – made glad demonstration of their feelings. In the evening Sauchiehall Street and Renfield Street were gay with crowds of all sorts and conditions. In the absence of military bands a brave effort was made to impart a melodic note to the jubilations by solo cornet and melodeon players and by solitary pipers. Now and again an unexpected bugle note was added, and the happy discord was increased by the clanging of the impatient warning bell of the tramway cars as they were driven through the surging crowds.

The city was fortunate in possessing a natural rallying point for the celebrations in George Square. It was the rendezvous, the *Herald* continued, 'of many thousands who sought to vent their feelings … the centre of our civic life and has been the theatre of numerous pageants of peace and war'. Observers recalled the 'stirring and patriotic scenes associated with the march-past of our city battalions prior to leaving the city for the battle fronts' and many also recollected the sad depletion of these same battalions. Glasgow marked the occasion in traditional fashion: by the peal of bells on the Cross steeple playing 'Rule Britannia' and the 'Marseillaise', and less familiarly, by the pair of aeroplanes which appeared over George Square, 'gracefully manoeuvring and releasing fire-balls to the delight of the dense throng who witnessed the display'.

Only a few weeks after the armistice, writers were beginning to publish works that were inspired by and looked back on the whole experience. One Scots novel in this category, which looked back over the war years and gave a flavour of Glasgow during the dark days of 1917, was *Mr Standfast*, the third of John Buchan's Richard Hannay stories, quickly published in 1918. This exciting novel has a section in which Glaswegians are portrayed carrying on in wartime with political disputes and industrial unrest much as they had done in peacetime. There is a typically Buchanesque description of a political meeting that is almost a fictional equivalent of the real visit paid by Lloyd George to the city (described in Chapter 8). Hannay visits wartime Glasgow in 1917 – a year before the time that Buchan was writing – and becomes involved in an uproarious political meeting called to create a branch of the 'British Council of Workmen and Soldiers'. This Soviet-style body also obviously has echoes of events actually happening in Russia at the time of the novel's setting. Although without the bloodletting of events in the real revolutionary Russia, Buchan's fictional Glasgow meeting rapidly degenerates into a chaotic ending – or 'rammy' to use a Glasgow expression. Hannay describes his arrival at the meeting hall:

As soon as we reached the platform I saw that there was going to be trouble. The hall was packed to the door, and in all the front half there was the kind of audience I expected to see – working men of the political type who before the war would have thronged to party meetings. But not all the crowd at the back had come to listen. Some were scallawags, some looked like better-class clerks out for a spree, and there was a fair quantity of khaki. There were also one or two gentlemen not strictly sober.

The chairman began by putting his foot in it. He said we were there tonight to protest against the continuation of the war and to form a branch of the new British Council of Workmen and Soldiers. He told them with a fine mixture of metaphors that we had got to take the reins into our own hands, for the men who were running the war had their own axes to grind and were marching to oligarchy through the blood of the workers. He added that we had no quarrel with Germany half as bad as we had with our own capitalists. He looked forward to the day when British soldiers would leap from their trenches and extend the hand of friendship to their German comrades.

John Buchan, *Mr Standfast*

Well, of course that did not happen in the First World War, and Scotland did not have a revolution – despite stirring events like the 'tuppence an hour' strike of 1915 and the Glasgow housewives' rent strike in the same year. One of the placards held aloft by the well-organised women and children, in the latter demonstration, read:

While my father is a prisoner in Germany, the landlord is attacking our home.

The casualties of the war have been calculated at around one tenth of the adult male population, but by its end the Glasgow working class had in a sense completed their political education. They had closed ranks for the duration, but in future their votes would be reserved for their own ends. Socialist realism had been confirmed as the predominant temper of the people of Glasgow.

Curiously, Buchan's passage about extending friendship to 'German comrades' was in an odd way a prediction of events at the end of the Second World War. In the century's second mammoth conflict it took the combined efforts of the Allies, with of course the Soviet Union, to grind down their

'German comrades'. In truth, as well as in fiction, Glasgow always had a special affinity with their Soviet comrades – at least that is what was suggested by the slogans daubed on walls and on roadways. But with the 'Cold War' and new lines being drawn, the day did come when British soldiers would, through NATO, 'extend the hand of friendship' to their former enemies.

In the course of what Angus Calder called 'The People's War' the citizens of Glasgow underwent even more privations and hardships, but at the end of the war they were probably more united than they had been at the end of the First World War. As the 1945 polls showed, and in contrast to the General Election of 1918, they were also very clear about the kind of post-war world and the kind of political leadership they wanted to see.

Once again, though, there were the expressions of public rejoicing at victory, and they were in the plural, because Glasgow showed its determination that a good party didn't have to wait for the official say so. There was more than one VE Day, because in Glasgow there were unofficial celebrations. One headline read: 'Midnight Frolics in Glasgow'. There were coloured lights in George Square and three tons of empty bottles. Glaswegians in the city centre had had a foretaste of the celebrations when floodlighting at the City Chambers was switched on on the eve of VE Day. A group of a hundred or more young folk had a try-out of their vocal powers in 'I Belong to Glasgow'. Newspapers also carried their first weather bulletins since 1939 – because during the period of hostilities this had been classified information that might have assisted enemy aircraft.

Just over a week after VE Day on 8 May, 1945 (VJ day was celebrated later on August 15), Glasgow's official victory parade was held in the city centre, with the various units, including the Home Guard and junior organisations, assembling at Blythswood Square and then marching downhill to the saluting base at George Square. The *Herald* described the scene:

> Taking the salute was Mr James Welsh, Lord Provost ... Fighting men in particular were accorded a welcome which was in the best traditions of the city of Glasgow and a special cheer was reserved for the Army [representatives] led by a Scottish major. The cap badges of three famous Scottish regiments who recently distinguished themselves in the fighting for Bremen led the rankers.

Other celebrations, such as those of the Boys' Brigade, attracted massive attendances. The BB thanksgiving service was held in Hampden Park and was attended by 9,000 boys and 25,000 spectators. The city's other great rallying point, Hampden, was at that time the biggest stadium in Europe and had hosted a number of Victory internationals and other morale-raising events during the war years.

With the end of the celebrations there began the long slog towards regeneration. Post-war reconstruction became a real possibility because of extensive pre-planning by Ernest Bevin's ministry, and was co-ordinated in Scotland by the energetic and charismatic Tom Johnston. In a series of ground-breaking speeches made within days of VE Day Bevin described the procedures for large-scale demobilisation of forces men and women, and then moved on to the immense task of re-deploying the national workforce, or 'Civil Employment', as he called it. Some wide-ranging points covered in just one of his *tour de force* speeches were reported in the Glasgow press:

- The call-up to the forces would go on. For a number of years there would be some form of national service.
- Women could continue to volunteer for the auxiliary forces, but no woman would be called up compulsorily.
- Married women and women with household responsibilities would be leaving industry in substantial numbers now the European war was over. They had done their bit and it would be wrong to compel them to remain, but he still asked them to respond to the national call where they could.
- Training within industry would continue. This country must never again, for its own sheer defence, let training and skilled personnel fall to the level of 1939.
- There had been risks taken by civilians in employment as well as by those in uniform, and a man could not be placed on one side merely because he had been retained in civilian employment. (This was a clause that had special resonance for Glasgow and Clydeside, where a high proportion of men had worked in reserved occupations.)
- Men would not be allowed to stand outside Labour Exchanges for weeks and months.
- Within three weeks of a man signing on ... if there was nothing doing, he would be trained for something else.

Johnston and Bevin's wartime programmes assisted moves towards identification of national priorities, e.g. nationalisation of major industries and public services, welfare state and full employment. At the General Election of July 1945 Glasgow duly delivered its part of the Labour landslide. Bob Crampsey's trenchant observation was:

GLASGOW: A CITY AT WAR

The Labour Party had won an astonishing victory and readers of the *Daily Express* were thunderstruck. The Conservatives had been humiliated and after the first dazed expectations of a Soviet had not been realised, it became apparent that they had deserved abundantly to be humiliated. Their campaign had been an affront to the voters and had consisted of nothing more than carrying the Prime Minister around like some form of primitive ju-ju ... men and women who had been torn away from their families for up to six years had not suffered as they had suffered to be given more of the same.

Bob Cramsey, *The Young Civilian*

A suitable postscript or epilogue comes from one of Glasgow's favourite forms of communal experience – the cinema or picture house. The Glaswegians' love of 'the pictures' remained unflagging throughout the war years and cinema audiences in vast numbers reacted with joy to the news of the surrender of most of the German forces in north Germany. An audience of about 2,000 in the Coliseum Cinema in Sauchiehall Street greeted with cheers the news flash passed to them from the stage, 'at the close of the showing of a cartoon'. Other films packing them in around that time included Deanna Durbin in *Can't Help Singing*. A reviewer commented:

> It is pure musical comedy, with no troubles about a plot – certainly with none of the melodrama into which Miss Durbin fitted so uneasily in 'Christmas Holiday' – it has tunes by Jerome Kern; and it is in the gaudiest possible Technicolor.

Maybe so, but for many of the citizens of Glasgow the next few years were to be more drab than 'technicolor', and within a few months audiences like these would boo newsreel images of Winston Churchill, great wartime leader now precipitately transformed into leader of His Majesty's Opposition.

Fig. 126

Another photograph showing stirring events in Glasgow's George Square. The crowd is listening to an address from Lord Provost James Welsh, after he had taken the salute at the Cenotaph. In the middle ground, is a large communal air-raid shelter. *(The Daily Record)*